A POCKET GUIDE TO . . .

Charles Darwin

His life and impact

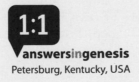

Petersburg, Kentucky, USA

Copyright ©2009 Answers in Genesis–US. All rights reserved. No part of this book may be used or reproduced in any manner whatsoever without written permission from the publisher. For more information write: Answers in Genesis, PO Box 510, Hebron, KY 41048

Sixth printing August 2012

ISBN: 1-60092-256-2

All Scripture quotations are taken from the New King James Version. Copyright ©1982 by Thomas Nelson, Inc. Used by permission. All rights reserved.

Printed in China

www.answersingenesis.org

Table of Contents

Introduction

There is much misunderstanding about Charles Darwin. Some consider him to be an evil man who sought to destroy Christianity. Others see him as the man who ushered in an era of scientific discovery and an understanding of the origin of life on earth, freeing humanity from bondage to ancient myths.

As you read through these chapters, the life and impact of Darwin will be presented. In the section on Darwin's life, the events that shaped his thinking are presented in a simple manner.

The section on science presents an analysis of the scientific claims of Darwin. Looking at Darwin's claims from a biblical perspective reveals inconsistencies not presented in the media and textbooks. If you have never examined the science from this perspective, you owe it to yourself to do so.

The last set of chapters explains the impact that Darwin's ideas have had on the world. Darwin's influence on racism, economics, and the role and purpose of humanity cannot be denied. But, do you know what those influences are? Whether you are a Christian or an atheist, an understanding of how Darwin's ideas have shaped history is important.

Timeline

Darwin's early life and education

- Charles Robert Darwin was born February 12, 1809 in Shrewsbury, England to a wealthy family.

- Darwin's mother, Susannah, died in 1817 when he was just 8.

- Beginning in 1818, Darwin attended Shrewsbury Grammar school with his older brother Erasmus under the direction of Reverend Samuel Butler.

- In 1825, his father Robert pulled him from the school and Darwin assisted his father at his medical practice.

- Darwin joined his brother Erasmus at the University of Edinburgh to study medicine in the fall of 1825.

- During his second year of medical school, Darwin began a friendship with Robert Grant who explained to him the evolutionary ideas of Lamarck.

- In the spring of 1827, Darwin left medical school and entered Christ's College at Cambridge in the winter of 1827 to study for the clergy. His brother Erasmus was also there to finish his schooling in medicine.

- Darwin did not take his studies seriously, but spent time collecting beetles and reading Shakespeare.

- In 1828, Darwin was introduced to Reverend John Stevens Henslow. Darwin took a strong interest in Henslow's lectures and began thinking of a career in the natural sciences.

- From 1829, Darwin doubted his career as a clergyman and did not take his studies seriously. Darwin studied Greek and Latin, as well as William Paley's works.

- In 1831, Darwin passed his exams and later attended geology lectures from Adam Sedgwick. Professor Sedgwick gave Darwin a crash course in field geology in the summer.

The *Beagle* voyage

- In August of 1831, Darwin was invited to be the naturalist aboard the *HMS Beagle*—an offer he readily accepted.

- While aboard the *Beagle*, Darwin read *Principles of Geology* by Charles Lyell. This book promoted an old-age, uniformitarian view of geology.

- Darwin was the companion of Captain Robert FitzRoy, a Christian who later rejected Darwin's ideas on evolution.

- The *Beagle* was on a surveying mission, which allowed Darwin time to venture inland in South America and other stops. He detailed the geology of these areas in his journals.

- Darwin collected many specimens of birds, animals, fish, and fossils and had them shipped back to Cambridge, along with his journals.

- The *Beagle* sailed up the coast of South America, eventually reaching the Galápagos Islands in September of 1835. They remained there until November, setting sail for Tahiti.

- After stops in Tahiti, New Zealand, Australia, Mauritius, Africa, as well as many other stops, they returned to England in October of 1936.

Years before *Origin of Species*

- Darwin interacted with many members of the scientific elite including Charles Lyell, Richard Owen, and Charles Babbage while his specimens were being studied by various naturalists.

- In 1837, John Gould concluded that the bird species that Darwin found on the Galápagos Islands were all finches with beak variations. Darwin began to formulate his ideas on change within and between species. Fearing that his idea of transmutation would be considered heretical, Darwin kept his ideas relatively private.

- Darwin began experiencing stomach and heart problems—these plagued him for the remainder of his life.

- In 1838, Darwin began studying the breeding of domestic animals to better understand how change occurred.

- Darwin read the work of Thomas Malthus describing how humans would struggle for resources as populations grew. Darwin adapted these ideas to animals.

- In 1839, Darwin married his cousin, Emma Wedgwood, receiving a small fortune from the family. This money was wisely invested ensuring that Darwin would not have to work for the rest of his life.

- Darwin took on a reclusive lifestyle to avoid triggering his health problems.

- In May of 1839, a three-volume narrative of the voyages of the *Beagle* was published, followed by his books on the geology of his voyages and the formation of coral reefs.

- William Erasmus was born to Charles and Emma in 1839.

- Anne Elizabeth was born in March 1841.

- In 1842, Darwin had written down his basic theory of the descent of animals through a process of natural selection. He decided not to make his ideas public so that he would not be considered an atheist, among other reasons.

- Mary Eleanor was born in September 1842, but died shortly after. Henrietta was born in September 1843.

- In late 1843, Darwin's five-volume work on the zoology of his *Beagle* voyage was published and Joseph Dalton Hooker became Darwin's research associate.

- In 1845, George was born into the family.

- In 1847, Darwin began working on a comprehensive study of barnacles to establish his credibility.

- Francis was born in August 1848 and Darwin's father, Robert, died in November. Charles was too ill to attend the funeral.

- Leonard was born into the family in January 1850 and Annie became very ill that summer. Annie died in April of 1851.

- In 1853, Darwin met Thomas Huxley and became friends with Herbert Spencer, with whom he spent time discussing human evolution.

- Darwin returned to work on his transmutation ideas and invited a group of scientists to Down House in April of 1856—there was a mixed reception as he presented his ideas.

- An essay by Alfred Russel Wallace on evolution of new species was sent to Lyell. Darwin was not impressed by it.

- Charles Waring was born into the family in December of 1856 but died in June of 1858.

- In June of 1858, Darwin received another paper by Wallace that contained many ideas similar to Darwin's. Wallace believed the process was guided by a higher power while Darwin believed the process acted without goals or guidance.

- On July 1, 1858, Darwin's and Wallace's papers on natural selection and the transmutation of species were read to a mixed review at the Linnaean Society in London.

- Darwin completed his book, and *On the Origin of Species by means of Natural Selection* was published and went on sale November 22, 1859.

Years after *Origin of Species*

- Thomas Huxley and Joseph Hooker took up the cause of Darwin and promoted his ideas in journals, influencing many in the scientific community.

- Richard Owen and Bishop Wilberforce fought fiercely against the Darwinian ideas, specifically on the grounds of morality and biblical truths.

- By 1863, *Origin* had been translated into French, German, Dutch, and Italian.

- Charles Lyell published a book on the ancient origin of man, though he did not directly connect his ideas to Darwinism.

- Ernst Haeckel paid a visit to Down House in 1866. Haeckel created fraudulent drawings to promote evolution.

- In 1866, Herbert Spencer coined the term "survival of the fittest" to avoid a selector acting in natural selection.

- Darwin's evolutionary ideas were directly applied to humans in his book *Descent of Man* which was published in March of 1871 along with a second volume on sexual selection.

- Darwin continued to study and write on many topics including orchid fertilization by insects, carnivorous plants, emotions in animals and humans, and many other topics.

- April 19, 1882, Charles Darwin died at Down House; he was buried in Westminster Abbey.

(Information primarily from www.aboutdarwin.com.)

Darwin's Personal Struggle with Evil

by Roger W. Sanders

*T*he doctor tries to look away as he says, "I'm sorry. I've done all I can. Your daughter is dying."

How would you respond? "God, this is hard to bear. Please give me eyes to see from Your perspective. Take my despair and turn it into joy." Or would you say, "God, why are You doing this to my family; what has this little girl done to deserve this?" Even born-again Christians struggle with pain and suffering.

But what if you had never placed your personal faith in Jesus Christ? Would you be more inclined to cry out, "What kind of God are You? This is all Your fault. I'm not sure I can still believe You exist."

That was Darwin's situation. He was 42 years old and his 10-year-old daughter, Anne, who had developed such a strong emotional connection with him, the joy of his life, lay dying. Her physical trauma hadn't appeared suddenly. Less than a year earlier, she developed a stomach illness like the one that had plagued him for 12 years. But hers was more severe, more feverish, came more often, and lasted longer. Likewise, doctors were puzzled by its cause. He took her to the health retreat where he had received the most help, but she found no relief.

At the end he stayed close at her side, at times relapsing into his own illness. After days of writhing with agony, she wasted away and passed into a coma before slipping irretrievably from her sobbing father.

Darwin's faith was not in Jesus Christ, only in what he could see, touch, and understand. Perhaps more than any other scientist of his time, this hurting father came to understand the evil that really exists in the natural world—"red in tooth and claw" as the poet Lord Tennyson described it. The death of Anne just made the evil touch him personally. As far as we know, it also made him turn away from God once and for all.

Just how profoundly he came to reject God is evident from this private message to his family, penned late in life and intended to be read after his death: "I can indeed hardly see how anyone ought to wish Christianity to be true; for if so the plain language of the text seems to show that the men who do not believe, and this would include my father, brother and almost all my best friends, will be everlastingly punished. And this is a damnable doctrine." Apparently, he understood the New Testament doctrine of salvation through the substitutionary death of Christ but did not believe it.

The blame for his turning away must fall partly on the church and the theologians and scientists who, decades before Anne's death, had already given up a biblical view of history. Adam's Fall and the Flood no longer had meaning as real events that shaped our world. The church foolishly explained that God created parasites to prod men to cleanliness, and mice to feed cats. The cat's capture of a mouse makes both the cat and the mouse "happy."

Without the Bible's explanation that Adam's sin brought death and a curse on the world, there is no satisfying answer to why evil exists. We also have no logical foundation to explain why Jesus needed to come to earth as a divine "second Adam" to defeat death (Romans 5:12–14; 1 Corinthians 15:44–49). The church failed to give Darwin a satisfying answer for the sight of a snake devouring a fallen baby bird or the pain of losing his daughter. Those in the church who claimed that God brought Adam's "very good" world into existence through millions of years of death and suffering made God out to be an ogre and a liar.

Darwin simply was unable to resolve suffering and death with a God who is good, just, and merciful. For him, the "Creator" was distant, caring little whether the world was very good or very bad. Rejecting the biblical view, he reasoned that death and suffering were integral to operation of the present world and had always existed.

Darwin proposed a new natural law—natural selection—which assumed that death has operated from the beginning. With this naturalistic, impersonal force of natural selection, he found a substitute for the God of the Bible, who is the Creator of all life-forms, the eternal Judge of sin, and the only possible Redeemer of fallen mankind and of our corrupted world.

 **Roger Sanders** earned his PhD in botany from the University of Texas. Currently, he is an associate professor of science at Bryan College, and is assistant director of CORE (Center for Origins Research).

Darwin—Unwittingly a "Creationist"

by Jason Lisle

Evolutionists often attempt to use observational science—arguments from biology, paleontology, geology, or even astronomy—to support their belief. But the really interesting thing is that they base all their arguments on principles that ultimately come from biblical creation! As strange as it may sound, evolutionists must unwittingly assume that creation is true in order to argue against it. That means that Darwin was (in a sense) a "creationist." All evolutionists must borrow the principles of biblical creation in order to do science (even though they would deny this). Here is why.

The Bible provides the foundation for an orderly universe

To do science, certain things must be true. The universe must be logical and have some organization to it. Moreover, the human mind must be capable of rational thought—capable of considering the various alternatives and then choosing the best. But if evolution were true, then we would have no reason to expect either of these conditions. If this world were nothing but a cosmic accident, if our brains were nothing but rearranged pond scum, then why would they be able to understand the universe?

On the other hand, a biblical creationist has every reason to expect scientific inquiry to be possible. The Bible teaches that God made the universe and the human mind, so we would expect these two things to "go together." Moreover, since God gave Adam the responsibility to care for creation, it makes sense that He would have given Adam the ability to understand the natural world.

The Bible is the foundation for logic

Logical reasoning itself only makes sense in a biblical worldview. To make a logical argument about anything, we have to use laws of logic. But if the universe is just matter in motion (as many evolutionists believe), laws of logic wouldn't exist since laws of logic are not made of matter. Laws of logic are "rules" that help us distinguish correct from incorrect forms of reasoning. But in an evolutionary universe, why should there be a standard for reasoning, and who is to say what that standard is? How could we ever really know for certain the laws of logic?

In the biblical creation worldview, however, laws of logic make sense. They reflect the thinking of God who upholds the entire universe by His power. God is our standard for correct thinking because all truth is in Him. We can know about laws of logic because God has made us in His image and has revealed some of His thoughts to us in His Word. We can expect laws of logic to be universally true and never change because they stem from the nature of God. So, when evolutionists such as Charles Darwin attempt to use science and logic, they reveal the fact that in their heart of hearts they know the God of creation.

The Bible makes sense of rules of behavior

Additionally, evolutionists believe in a moral code: a standard for how we should think and behave. But the idea of a moral code goes back to biblical creation. Since God has created us, He has the right to set the rules of behavior. In fact, the Bible tells us that the law is written on our hearts. However, if people were just complex chemicals and our decisions were just chemical reactions, then people wouldn't have any genuine choice in what they do. If we were not created by God, then any moral code invented by people would just be arbitrary opinion.

This doesn't mean that evolutionists don't act morally, but those who reject biblical creation have no ultimate basis for their morality. So when evolutionists tell us how to think or behave, they are acting as if they believe in creation. Their actions reveal that they embrace an objective moral code, even though they have no basis for it in their professed worldview.

The fact that evolutionists believe in science, rationality, and morality is inconsistent with their professed belief in evolution. This shows that in their hearts, they really know the God whose Word they are attacking, even though they verbally deny this. They "suppress" the truth, as the Scripture teaches (Romans 1:18–25).

From Darwin to Dawkins, all evolutionists have relied upon their suppressed knowledge of the God of creation—as evidenced by their belief in science, logic, and morality. As a result of their failure to honor God or thank Him, their thinking is reduced to futile speculations (Romans 1:21).

The notion of particles-to-people evolution is just one example of mankind's speculations. But people cannot consistently function rationally with such a futile way of thinking. In their effort to construct arguments against biblical creation, evolutionists must unwittingly rely on the concepts that can come only from biblical creation.

All knowledge is in Christ (Colossians 2:3). So anyone who wants to be consistently rational and scientific must submit to Him first (Proverbs 1:7). Christians who understand and embrace this truth have a powerful tool for defending the Christian faith and reaching the unsaved with the gospel.

The next time someone tries to condemn the biblical view of origins using arguments from biology or other sciences, just remind him that scientific arguments make consistent, logical sense only when reality is understood from a biblical worldview, beginning with creation. Equipped with this powerful apologetics method, you can point out how all evolutionists must, in reality, assume that creation is true in order to attempt to logically argue against it.

Beginning your discussions on the Scripture's authority, you will stand on solid ground (Matthew 7:24–29).

Jason Lisle earned his PhD in astrophysics from the University of Colorado at Boulder. As one of the few creationist astrophysicists doing research today, he works full-time in AiG's new Research Division. He also programs and designs the shows for the Creation Museum's Stargazers Room planetarium.

Is Natural Selection the Same Thing as Evolution?

by Georgia Purdom

Here is a hypothetical conversation between a biblical creationist (C) and an evolutionist (E) as they discuss some recent scientific news:

E: Isn't the new finding regarding coat color change in mice a wonderful example of evolution in action?

C: No, I think it's a good example of natural selection in action, which is merely selecting information that already exists.

E: Well, what about antibiotic resistance in bacteria? Don't you think that's a good example of evolution?

C: No, you seem to be confusing the terms "evolution" and "natural selection."

E: But natural selection is the primary mechanism that drives evolution.

C: Natural selection doesn't drive molecules-to-man evolution; you are giving natural selection a power that it does not have—one that can supposedly add new information to the genome, as molecules-to-man evolution requires. But natural selection simply can't do that because it works with information that already exists.

Natural selection is an observable process that is often purported to be the underlying mechanism of unobservable molecules-to-man evolution. The concepts are indeed different, though some mistakenly interchange the two. So let's take a closer look. There are two major questions to answer:

1. How do biblical creationists rightly view the observable phenomenon of natural selection?
2. Could this process cause the increase in genetic information necessary for molecules-to-man evolution?

What is natural selection?

Below are some definitions evolutionists use to define "natural selection." The problem biblical creationists have with these definitions lies mostly in their misapplication, as noted by the bolded phrases.

Evolutionary change based on the differential reproductive success of individuals within a species.[1]

The process by which genetic traits are passed on to each successive generation. Over time, natural selection helps species become better adapted to their environment. Also known as "survival of the fittest," **natural selection is the driving force behind the process of evolution**.[2]

The process in nature by which, according to **Darwin's theory of evolution**, only the organisms best adapted to their environment tend to survive and transmit their genetic characters in increasing numbers to succeeding generations while those less adapted tend to be eliminated (**also see evolution**).[3]

From a creationist perspective natural selection is a process whereby organisms possessing specific characteristics (reflective of their genetic makeup) survive better than others in a given environment or under a given selective pressure (i.e., antibiotic resistance in bacteria). Those with certain characteristics live, and those without them diminish in number or die.

The problem for evolutionists is that natural selection is nondirectional—should the environment change or the selective pressure be removed, those organisms with previously selected for characteristics are typically less able to deal with the changes and may be selected against because their genetic information has decreased—more on this later. Evolution of the molecules-to-man variety requires directional change. Thus, the term "evolution" cannot be rightly used in the context of describing what natural selection can accomplish.

What is evolution?

This term has many definitions just as "natural selection" does. Much of the term's definition depends on the context in which the word "evolution" is used. Below are some recent notable definitions of evolution (note the bold phrases).

Unfolding in time of a predictable or prepackaged sequence in an inherently, or at least **directional manner**.[4]

The theory that all life forms are **descended** from **one or several common ancestors** that were present on early earth, **three to four billion years** ago.[5]

The "Big Idea" [referring to evolution] is that living things (species) are related to one another through **common ancestry** from earlier forms that differed from them. Darwin called this "**descent with modification**," and it is still the best definition of evolution we can use, **especially with members of the general public and with young learners**.[6]

All of these definitions give the same basic idea that evolution is *directional* in producing all the life-forms on earth today from one or several ancestral life-forms billions of years ago. The last definition is especially intriguing because it indicates that an ambiguous definition of evolution should be used with the public and with children. Most creationists would agree partially with the idea of "descent with modification" in that species we have today look different from the original kinds that God created (i.e., the great variety of dogs we have now compared to the original created dog kind). The advantage with using such a broad definition for evolution is that it can include any and all supporting models of evolution (such as traditional Darwinism, neo-Darwinism, punctuated equilibrium, etc.) and can spark the least amount of controversy in the public eye.

Historical background on the discovery of natural selection

Many people give credit to Charles Darwin for formulating the theory of natural selection as described in his book *On the Origin of Species*. Few realize that Darwin only popularized the idea and actually borrowed it from several other people, especially a creationist by the name of Edward Blyth. Blyth published several articles describing the process of natural selection in *Magazine of Natural History* between 1835 and 1837—a full 22 years before Darwin published his book. It is also known that Darwin had copies of these magazines and that parts of *On the Origin of Species* are nearly verbatim from Blyth's articles.[7]

Blyth, however, differed from Darwin in his starting assumptions. Blyth believed in God as the Creator, rather than the blind forces of nature. He believed that God created original kinds, that all modern species descended from those kinds, and that natural selection acted by conserving rather than originating. Blyth also believed that man was a separate creation from animals. This is especially important since humans are made in the image of God, an attribute that cannot be applied to animals (Genesis 1:27). Blyth seemed to view natural selection as a mechanism designed directly or indirectly by God to allow His creation to survive in a post-Fall, post-Flood world. This is very different from Darwin's view. Darwin wrote, "What a book a devil's chaplain might write on the clumsy, wasteful, blundering low and horridly cruel works of nature."[8]

Is natural selection biblical?

It is important to see natural selection as a mechanism that God used to allow organisms to deal with their changing environments in a sin-cursed world—especially after the Flood. God foreknew that the Fall and the Flood were going to happen, and so He designed organisms with a great amount of genetic diversity that could be selected for or against, resulting in certain characteristics depending on the circumstances. Whether this information was initially part of the original design during Creation Week before the Fall or was added, in part, at the Fall (as a part of the punishment of man and the world by God),[9] we can't be certain. Regardless, the great variety of information in the original created kinds can only be attributed to an intelligence—God.

In addition, natural selection works to preserve the genetic viability of the original created kinds by removing from the population those with severely deleterious/lethal characteristics. Natural selection, acting on genetic information, is the primary mechanism that explains how organisms could have survived after the Fall and Flood when the world changed drastically from God's original creation.

Let me take a moment to clarify an important theological point so there is no confusion. Death entered the world as the result of sin. Death, therefore, is in the world as a punishment for man's disobedience to God, and it should remind us that the world is sin-cursed and needs a Savior. Death is not a good thing but is called an enemy (1 Corinthians 15:26).

But recall that God, in His infinite wisdom, can make good come out of anything, and death is no exception. God is able to make good come out of even death itself. Natural selection, though fueled by death, helps the population by getting rid of genetic defects, etc. In the same way, without death Christ wouldn't have conquered it and been glorified in His Resurrection.

So what can natural selection accomplish and not accomplish? The table on the next page displays some of the main points.

Natural Selection Can	**Natural Selection Cannot**
1. Decrease genetic information.	1. Increase or provide new genetic information.
2. Allow organisms to survive better in a given environment.	2. Allow organisms to evolve from molecules to man.
3. Act as a "selector."	3. Act as an "originator."
4. Support creation's "orchard" of life.	4. Support evolutionary "tree" of life.

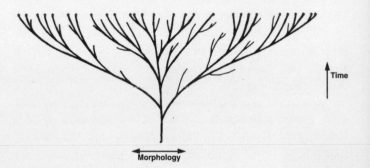

The evolutionary tree, which postulates that all today's species are descended from one common ancestor (which itself evolved from nonliving chemicals).

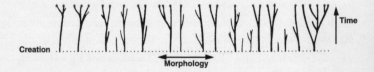

The creationist orchard,[10] which shows that diversity has occurred within the original Genesis kinds over time.[11]

Natural selection and dogs

Let's illustrate the possibilities and limitations of natural selection using the example of varying fur length of dogs (designed variation).

There are many different dog species—some with long fur and some with short fur. The original dog kind, most likely resembling today's wolf, had several variants of the gene for fur length. L will be the variant of the gene representing long fur, and S will be the variant of the gene representing short fur.

The original dog kind most likely would have been a mixture of the genes specifying fur length, including both L and S. Because of this makeup, they also most likely had the characteristic of medium fur length. When the original kind (LS dogs) mated, their genetic variability could be seen in their offspring in three ways—LL for long fur, LS for medium fur, and SS for short fur.

If two long-fur dogs then mated, the only possible outcome for the offspring is LL, long fur. As can be seen in the example below, the long-fur dogs have lost the S gene variant and are thus not capable of producing dogs with short fur or medium fur. This loss may be an advantage if these long-fur dogs live in an area with cold temperatures. The long-fur dogs would then be naturally selected for, as they would survive better in the given environment. Eventually, the majority of this area's dog population would have long fur.

However, the loss of the S variant could be a disadvantage to the long-fur dogs if the climate became warmer or if the dogs moved to a warmer climate. Because of their decreased genetic variety (no S gene), they would be unable to produce dogs with short fur, which would be needed to survive better in a warm environment. In this situation, the long-fur dogs would be naturally selected against and die.

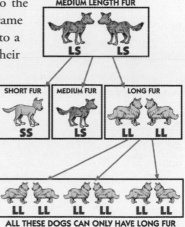

MEDIUM LENGTH FUR
LS   LS

SHORT FUR   MEDIUM FUR   LONG FUR
SS   LS   LL   LL

LL   LL   LL   LL   LL   LL
ALL THESE DOGS CAN ONLY HAVE LONG FUR

When the two dogs representing the dog kind came off Noah's Ark and began spreading across the globe, we can see how the variation favored some animals and not others.

Using the points from the table for what natural selection can accomplish (seen above), it can be seen that:

1. Through natural selection, genetic information (variety) was lost.

2. The long-fur dogs survive better in a cold environment; they are less able to survive in a warm environment and vice versa.

3. A particular characteristic in the dog population was selected for.

4. Dogs are still dogs since the variation is within the boundaries of "kind."

Natural selection of designed variation within the dog kind is not an example of evolution because it does not lead to the formation of a different kind of animal such as a horse, bear, or human. Instead, it is evidence of God's grace in supplying for His creation in the altered environments of a post-Fall, post-Flood world.

Natural selection and bacteria

Another example of natural selection is that of antibiotic resistance in bacteria. Such natural selection is commonly portrayed as evolution in action, but in this case, natural selection works in conjunction with mutation rather than designed variation.

Antibiotics are natural products produced by fungi and bacteria, and the antibiotics we use today are typically derivatives of those. Because of this relationship, it is not surprising that some bacteria would have resistance to certain antibiotics; they must do so to be competitive in their environment. In fact, if you took a sample of soil from outside your home, you would find antibiotic-resistant bacteria.

A bacterium can gain resistance through two primary ways:

1. By losing genetic information, and

2. By using a design feature built in to swap DNA—a bacterium gains resistance from another bacterium that has resistance.

Let's take a look at the first. Antibiotics usually bind a protein in the bacterium and prevent it from functioning properly, killing the bacteria. Antibiotic-resistant bacteria have a mutation in the DNA which codes for that protein. The antibiotic then cannot bind to the protein produced from the mutated DNA, and thus, the bacteria live. Although the bacteria can survive well in an environment with antibiotics, it has come at a cost. If the antibiotic-resistant bacteria are grown with the nonmutant bacteria in an environment without antibiotics, the nonmutant bacteria will live and the mutant bacteria will die. This is because the mutant bacteria produce a mutant protein that does not allow them to compete with other bacteria for necessary nutrients. The "supergerms" are really "superwimps."[12]

Let's clarify this some by looking at the bacteria *Helicobacter pylori*. Antibiotic-resistant *H. pylori* have a mutation that results in the loss of information to produce an enzyme. This enzyme normally converts an antibiotic to a poison, which causes death. But when the antibiotics are applied to the mutant *H. pylori*, these bacteria can live while the normal bacteria are killed. So by natural selection the ones that lost information survive and pass this trait along to their offspring.

Now let's take a look at the second method. A bacterium can get antibiotic resistance by gaining the aforementioned mutated DNA from another bacterium. Unlike you and me, bacteria can swap DNA. It is important to note that this is still not considered a gain of genetic information since the information already exists and that while the mutated DNA may be new to a particular bacterium, it is not new overall.

Using the points from the table for what natural selection can accomplish, it can be seen that:

1. Through mutation, genetic information was lost.

2. The antibiotic resistant bacteria *only* survive well in an

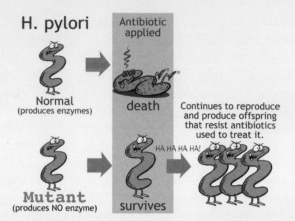

environment with antibiotics; they are less able to survive in the wild. (It is important to keep in mind that the gain of antibiotic resistance is not an example of a beneficial mutation but rather a beneficial outcome of a mutation in a given environment. These types of mutations are rare in other organisms as offspring are more limited in number; therefore, there is a greater need to preserve genetic integrity.)

3. A particular mutation in a bacterial population was selected for.

4. *H. pylori* is still *H. pylori*. No evolution has taken place to change it into something else—it's still the same bacteria with some variation.

Antibiotic resistance in bacteria, rather than being an example of evolution in action, is another example of natural selection seen properly from a biblical/creationist perspective.

Speciation—a possible outcome of natural selection

A species can be defined as a population of organisms produced by a parent population that has changed so significantly that it can no longer interbreed with the parent population. Using the example of dogs, it is possible that long-fur dogs might change sufficiently (other changes besides fur might also be selected for living in cold environments) to the point that they can no longer mate with short-fur or medium fur dogs.

Although evolutionists claim that speciation takes long periods of time (millions of years), they are often amazed at how fast species can be observed to form today. Speciation has been observed to occur in as little as a few years as seen in guppies, lizards, fruit flies, mosquitoes, finches, and mice.[13] This observation does not come as a surprise to creationists as all species alive in the past and today would have had to be produced in fewer than 6,000 years from the original created kinds. In fact, such processes (and perhaps other genetic factors) would have occurred rapidly after the Flood, producing variation within each kind. Such effects are largely responsible for generating the tremendous diversity seen in the living world.[14]

Speciation has never been observed to form an organism of a different kind, such as a dog species producing a cat. Speciation works *only* within a kind. Evolution requires natural selection and speciation to give rise to new kinds from a former kind (e.g., dinosaurs evolving into birds). Speciation, however, leads to a loss of information, not the gain of information required by evolution. Thus, speciation as a possible outcome of natural selection cannot be used as a mechanism for molecules-to-man evolution.

Conclusion

When discussing natural selection as a possible mechanism for evolution, it is important to define terms. Evolutionists and biblical creationists view these terms differently, but it comes down to how we interpret the evidence in light of our foundation. Do we view natural selection using God's Word as our foundation, or do we use man's truth as our foundation?

The creationist view of natural selection is supported biblically and scientifically. Natural selection is a God-ordained process that allows organisms to survive in a post-Fall, post-Flood world. It is an observable reality that occurs in the present and takes advantage of the variations within the kinds and works to preserve the genetic viability of the kinds.

Simply put, the changes that are observed today show variation within the created kind—a horizontal change. For a molecules-to-man evolutionary model, there must be a change from one kind into another—a vertical change. This is simply not observed. We have never seen a bacterium like *H. pylori* give rise to something like a dog. Instead, we simply observe variations within each created kind.

Evolution requires an increase in information that results in a directional movement from molecules to man. Natural selection cannot be a mechanism for evolution because it results in a decrease in information and is not directional. Speciation may occur as a result of natural selection, but it only occurs within a kind. Therefore, it is also not a mechanism for evolution but rather supports the biblical model.

Natural selection cannot be the driving force for molecules-to-man evolution when it does not have that power, nor should it be confused with molecules-to-man evolution. It is an observable phenomenon that preserves genetic viability and allows limited variation within a kind—nothing more, nothing less. It is a great confirmation of the Bible's history.

1. Michael A. Park, "*Introducing Anthropology: An Integrated Approach*, 2nd Ed., online glossary, McGraw-Hill, http://highered.mcgraw-hill.com/sites/0072549238/student_view0/glossary.html.

2. National Geographic, "Strange Days on Planet Earth Glossary," http://www.pbs.org/strangedays/glossary/N.html.

3. "Dinosaurs—glossary of terms," http://www.internal.schools.net.au/edu/lesson_ideas/dinosaurs/glossary.html.

4. Stephen J. Gould, "What does the dreaded 'E' word mean, anyway?" *Natural History* 109 no. 1 (2000): 28–44.

5. Denyse O'Leary, *By Design or by Chance?* (Kitchener, ON: Castle Quay, 2004), p. 7.

6. Eugenie C. Scott, "Creation or evolution?" http://www.ncseweb.org/resources/articles/6261_creation_or_evolution__1_9_2001.asp.

7. James M. Foard, "Edward Blyth and natural selection," The Darwin Papers, http://www.thedarwinpapers.com/oldsite/Number2/Darwin2Html.htm.

8. Charles Darwin, letter to Joseph Hooker, Darwin Archives, Cambridge University, July 13, 1856.

9. Ken Ham, ed., *New Answers Book* (Green Forest, AR: Master Books, 2006), pp. 259–270.

10. Illustration used with permission from Dr. Kurt Wise and Creation Science Fellowship of Pittsburgh from the 1990 ICC Proceedings, Bob Walsh editor, vol. 2, p. 358.

11. Creationists often refer to each kind as a *baramin*, from Hebrew *bara* = create and *min* = kind.

12. Carl Wieland, "Superbugs Not Super After All," *Creation*, June–August 1992, pp. 10–13.

13. David Catchpoole and Carl Wieland, "Speedy Species Surprise," *Creation*, March–May 2001, pp. 13–15, March 2001.

14. Carl Wieland, "Darwin's Finches," *Creation*, June–August 1992, pp. 22–23.

Georgia Purdom received her PhD in molecular genetics from Ohio State University in 2000. She is a member of the Human Anatomy and Physiology Society, American Society for Cell Biology, Creation Research Society, and American Society for Microbiology. Dr. Purdom has published papers in several scientific journals and is now engaged in full-time research, speaking, and writing on the topic of creation for Answers in Genesis.

Did Humans Really Evolve from Ape-like Creatures?

by David Menton

Television documentaries on human evolution abound. Some of the more popular in recent years have been *Walking with Cavemen* (2003) produced by BBC and aired on the Discovery Channel, *The Journey of Man: A Genetic Odyssey* (2003), produced by National Geographic and *Survivor: The Mystery of Us* (2005), also by National Geographic. All of these shows present as fact the story of human evolution from apelike creatures over the past several million years. They claim that anthropologists have found links in the human evolutionary chain and that scientists have "proven" evolution happens through DNA and other studies. But what is the real evidence for human evolution? What evidence are we not hearing? In this chapter, we will examine how anthropologists either make a man out of a monkey or make monkeys out of men. And once again, we'll conclude that the evidence points to the fact that man is a unique creation, made in the image of God.

Perhaps the most bitter pill to swallow for any Christian who attempts to "make peace" with Darwin is the presumed ape ancestry of man. Even many Christians who uncritically accept evolution as "God's way of creating" try to somehow elevate the origin of man, or at least his soul, above that of the beasts. Evolutionists attempt to soften the blow by assuring us that man didn't exactly evolve from apes (tailless monkeys) but rather from *apelike creatures*. This is mere semantics, however, as many of the presumed apelike ancestors of man are apes and have scientific names, which include the word *pithecus* (derived from the Greek meaning "ape"). The much-touted "human ancestor" commonly known as "Lucy," for example, has the scientific name *Australopithecus afarensis* (meaning "southern ape from the Afar triangle of Ethiopia"). But what does the Bible say about the origin of man, and what exactly is the scientific evidence that evolutionists claim for our ape ancestry?

Biblical starting assumptions

God tells us that on the same day He made all animals that walk on the earth (the sixth day), He created man separately in His own image with the intent that man would have dominion over every other living thing on earth (Genesis 1:26-28). From this it is clear that there is no animal that is man's equal, and certainly none his ancestor.

Thus when God paraded the animals by Adam for him to name, He observed that "for Adam there was not found an help meet for him" (Genesis 2:20). Jesus confirmed this uniqueness of men and women when He declared that marriage is to be between a man and a woman because "from the beginning of the creation God made them male and female" (Mark 10:6). This leaves no room for prehumans or for billions of years of cosmic evolution prior to man's appearance on the earth. Adam chose the very name "Eve" for his wife because he recognized that she would be "the mother of all living" (Genesis 3:20). The Apostle Paul stated clearly that man is not an animal: "All flesh is not the same flesh, but there is one kind of flesh of men, another flesh of animals, another of fish, and another of birds" (1 Corinthians 15:39).

Evolutionary starting assumptions

While Bible-believing Christians begin with the assumption that God's Word is true and that man's ancestry goes back only to a fully human Adam and Eve, evolutionists begin with the assumption that man has, in fact, evolved from apes. No paleoanthropologists (those who study the fossil evidence for man's origin) would dare to seriously raise the question, "Did man evolve from apes?" The only permissible question is "From which apes did man evolve?"

Since evolutionists generally do not believe that man evolved from any ape that is now living, they look to fossils of humans and apes to provide them with their desired evidence. Specifically, they look for any anatomical feature that looks "intermediate" (between that of apes and man). Fossil apes having such features are declared to be ancestral to man (or at least collateral relatives) and are called hominids. Living apes, on the other hand, are not considered to be hominids, but rather are called hominoids because they are only similar to humans but did not evolve into them. Nonetheless, evolutionists are willing to accept mere similarities between the fossilized bones of extinct apes and the bones of living men as "proof" of our ape ancestry.

What is the evidence for human evolution?

Though many similarities may be cited between living apes and humans, the only historical evidence that could support the ape ancestry of man must come from fossils. Unfortunately, the fossil record of man and apes is very sparse. Approximately 95% of all known fossils are marine invertebrates, about 4.7% are algae and plants, about 0.2% are insects and other invertebrates and only about 0.1% are vertebrates (animals with bones). Finally, only the smallest imaginable fraction of vertebrate fossils consists of primates (humans, apes, monkeys and lemurs).

Because of the rarity of fossil hominids, even many of those who specialize in the evolution of man have never actually seen an original hominid fossil, and far fewer have ever had the opportunity to handle or study one. Most scientific papers on human evolution are based on casts of original specimens (or even on published photos, measurements and descriptions of them).

Access to original fossil hominids is strictly limited by those who discovered them and is often confined to a few favored evolutionists who agree with the discoverers' interpretation of the fossil.

Since there is much more prestige in finding an ancestor of man than an ancestor of living apes (or worse yet, merely an extinct ape), there is immense pressure on paleoanthropologists to declare almost any ape fossil to be a "hominid." As a result, the living apes have pretty much been left to find their own ancestors.

Many students in our schools are taught human evolution (often in the social studies class!) by teachers having little knowledge of human anatomy, to say nothing of ape anatomy. But it is useless to consider the fossil evidence for the evolution of man from apes without first understanding the basic anatomical and functional differences between human and ape skeletons.

Jaws and teeth

Because of their relative hardness, teeth and jaw fragments are the most frequently found primate fossils. Thus, much of the evidence for the ape ancestry of man is based on similarities of teeth and jaws.

In contrast to man, apes tend to have incisor and canine teeth that are relatively larger than their molars. Ape teeth usually have thin enamel (the hardest surface layer of the tooth), while humans generally have thicker enamel. Finally, the jaws tend to be more U-shaped in apes and more parabolic in man.

The problem in declaring a fossil ape to be a human ancestor (i.e., a hominid) on the basis of certain humanlike features of the teeth is that some living apes have these same features and they are not considered to be ancestors of man. Some species of modern baboons, for example, have relatively small canines and incisors and relatively large molars. While most apes do have thin enamel, some apes such as the orangutans have relatively thick enamel. Clearly, teeth tell us more about an animal's diet and feeding habits than its supposed evolution. Nonetheless, thick enamel is one of the most commonly cited criteria for declaring an ape fossil to be a hominid.

Artistic imagination has been used to illustrate entire "apemen" from nothing more than a single tooth. In the early 1920s, the "apeman" *Hesperopithecus* (which consisted of a single tooth) was pictured in the *London Illustrated News* complete with the tooth's wife, children, domestic animals, and cave! Experts used this tooth, known as "Nebraska man," as proof for human evolution during the Scopes trial in 1925. In 1927 parts of the skeleton were discovered together with the teeth, and Nebraska man was found to really be an extinct peccary (wild pig)!

Skulls

Skulls are perhaps the most interesting primate fossils because they house the brain and give us an opportunity, with the help of imaginative artists, to look our presumed ancestors in the face. The human skull is easily distinguished from all living apes, though there are, of course, similarities.

The vault of the skull is large in humans because of their relatively large brain compared to apes. Even so, the size of the normal adult human brain varies over nearly a threefold range. These differences in size in the human brain do not correlate with intelligence. Adult apes have brains that are generally smaller than even the smallest of adult human brains and, of course, are not even remotely comparable in intelligence.

Perhaps the best way to distinguish an ape skull from a human skull is to examine it from a side view. From this perspective, the face of the human is nearly vertical, while that of the ape slopes forward from its upper face to its chin.

From a side view, the bony socket of the eye (the orbit) of an ape is obscured by its broad flat upper face. Humans, on the other hand, have a more curved upper face and forehead, clearly revealing the orbit of the eye from a side view.

Leg bones

The most eagerly sought-after evidence in fossil hominids is any anatomical feature that might suggest *bipedality* (the ability to walk on two legs). Since humans walk on two legs, any evidence of bipedality in fossil apes is considered by evolutionists to be compelling evidence for human ancestry. But we should bear in mind that the way an ape walks on two legs is entirely different from the way man walks on two legs. The distinctive human gait requires the complex integration of many skeletal and muscular features in our hips, legs and feet. Thus, evolutionists closely examine the hipbones (*pelvis*), thighbones (*femur*), leg bones (*tibia* and *fibula*) and foot bones of fossil apes in an effort to detect any anatomical features that might suggest bipedality.

Evolutionists are particularly interested in the angle at which the femur and the tibia meet at the knee (called the *carrying angle*). Humans are able to keep their weight over their feet while walking because their femurs converge toward the knees, forming a carrying angle of approximately 9 degrees with the tibia (in other words, we're sort of knock-kneed). In contrast, chimps and gorillas have widely separated straight legs with a carrying angle of essentially 0 degrees. These animals manage to keep their weight over their feet when walking by swinging their body from side to side in the familiar "ape walk."

Evolutionists assume that fossil apes with a high carrying angle (humanlike) were bipedal and thus evolving into man. Certain australopithecines (an apelike creature) are considered to have walked like us and thus to be our ancestors largely because they had a high carrying angle. But high carrying angles are not confined to humans—they are also found on some modern apes that walk gracefully on tree limbs and only clumsily on the ground.

Living apes with a high carrying angle (values comparable to man) include such apes as the orangutan and spider monkey—both adept tree climbers and capable of only an apelike bipedal gait on the ground. The point is that there are living tree-dwelling apes and monkeys with some of the same anatomical features that evolutionists consider to be definitive evidence for bipedality, yet none of these animals walks like man and no one suggests they are our ancestors or descendants.

Foot bones

The human foot is unique and not even close to the appearance or function of the ape foot. The big toe of the human foot is inline with the foot and does not jut out to the side like apes. Human toe bones are relatively straight rather than curved and grasping like ape toes.

While walking, the heel of the human foot first hits the ground, then the weight distribution spreads from the heel along the outer margin of the foot up to the base of the little toe. From the little toe it spreads inward across the base of the toes and finally pushes off from the big toe. No ape has a foot or push-off like that of a human; and thus, no ape is capable of walking with our distinctive human stride, or of making human footprints.

Hipbones

The pelvis (hipbones) plays a critically important role in walking, and the characteristic human gait requires a pelvis that is distinctly different from that of the apes. Indeed, one only has to examine the pelvis to determine if an ape has the ability to walk like a man.

The part of the hipbones that we can feel just under our belt is called the iliac blade. Viewed from above, these blades are curved forward like the handles of a steering yolk on an airplane. The iliac blades of the ape, in contrast, project straight out to the side like the handlebars of a scooter. It is simply not possible to walk like a human with an apelike pelvis. On this feature alone one can easily distinguish apes from humans.

Only three ways to make an "apeman"

Knowing from Scripture that God didn't create any apemen, there are only three ways for the evolutionist to create one.

1. Combine ape fossil bones with human fossilbones and declare the two to be one individual—a real "apeman."

2. Emphasize certain humanlike qualities of fossilized ape bones, and with imagination upgrade apes to be more humanlike.

3. Emphasize certain apelike qualities of fossilized human bones, and with imagination downgrade humans to be more apelike.

These three approaches account for *all* of the attempts by evolutionists to fill the unbridgeable gap between apes and men with fossil apemen.

Combining men and apes

The most famous example of an apeman proven to be a combination of ape and human bones is Piltdown man. In 1912, Charles Dawson, a medical doctor and an amateur paleontologist, discovered a mandible (lower jawbone) and part of a skull in a gravel pit near Piltdown, England. The jawbone was apelike but had teeth that showed wear similar to the human pattern. The skull, on the other hand, was very humanlike. These two specimens were combined to form what was called "Dawn man," which was calculated to be 500,000 years old.

The whole thing turned out to be an elaborate hoax. The skull was indeed human (about 500 years old), while the jaw was that of a modern female orangutan whose teeth had been obviously filed to crudely resemble the human wear pattern. Indeed, the long ape canine tooth was filed down so far that it exposed the pulp chamber, which was then filled in to hide the mischief. It would seem that any competent scientist examining this tooth would have concluded that it was either a hoax or the world's first root canal! The success of this hoax for over 50 years, in spite of the careful scrutiny of the best authorities in the world, led the human evolutionist Sir Solly Zuckerman to declare: "It is doubtful if there is any science at all in the search for man's fossil ancestry."[1]

Making man out of apes

Many apemen are merely apes that evolutionists have attempted to upscale to fill the gap between apes and men. These include all the australopithecines, as well as a host of other extinct apes such as *Ardipithecus, Orrorin, Sahelanthropus,* and *Kenyanthropus*. All have obviously ape skulls, ape pelvises and ape hands and feet. Nevertheless, australopithecines (especially *Australopithecus afarensis*) are often portrayed as having hands and feet identical to modern man, a ramrod-straight, upright posture and a human gait.

The best-known specimen of *A. afarensis* is the fossil commonly known as "Lucy." A life-like mannequin of "Lucy" in the *Living World* exhibit at the St. Louis Zoo shows a hairy humanlike female body with human hands and feet but with an obviously apelike head. The three-foot-tall Lucy stands erect in a deeply pensive pose with her right forefinger curled under her chin, her eyes gazing off into the distance as if she were contemplating the mind of Newton.

Few visitors are aware that this is a gross misrepresentation of what is known about the fossil ape *Australopithecus afarensis*. These apes are known to be long-armed knuckle-walkers with locking wrists. Both the hands and feet of this creature are clearly apelike. Paleoanthropologists Jack Stern and Randall Sussman[2] have reported that the hands of this species are "surprisingly similar to hands found in the small end of the pygmy chimpanzee-common chimpanzee range." They report that the feet, like the hands, are "long, curved and heavily muscled" much like those of living tree-dwelling primates. The authors conclude that no living primate has such hands and feet "for any purpose other than to meet the demands of full or part-time arboreal (tree-dwelling) life."

Despite evidence to the contrary, evolutionists and museums continue to portray Lucy (*A. afarensis*) with virtually human feet (though some are finally showing the hands with long curved fingers).

Making apes out of man

In an effort to fill the gap between apes and men, certain fossil *men* have been declared to be "apelike" and thus, ancestral to at least "modern" man. You might say this latter effort seeks to make a "monkey" out of man. Human fossils that are claimed to be "apemen" are generally classified under the genus *Homo* (meaning "self"). These include *Homo erectus*, *Homo heidelbergensis*, and *Homo neanderthalensis*.

The best-known human fossils are of Cro-Magnon man (whose marvelous paintings are found on the walls of caves in France) and Neanderthal man. Both are clearly human and have long been classified as *Homo sapiens*. In recent years, however, Neanderthal man has been downgraded to a different species— *Homo neanderthalensis*.

Neanderthal man was first discovered in 1856 by workmen digging in a limestone cave in the Neander valley near Dusseldorf, Germany. The fossil bones were examined by an anatomist (professor Schaafhausen) who concluded that they were human.

At first, not much attention was given to these finds, but with the publication of Darwin's *Origin of Species* in 1859, the search began for the imagined "apelike ancestors" of man. Darwinians argued that Neanderthal man was an apelike creature, while many critical of Darwin (like the great anatomist Rudolph Virchow) argued that Neanderthals were human in every respect, though some appeared to be suffering from rickets or arthritis.

Over 300 Neanderthal specimens have now been found scattered throughout most of the world, including Belgium, China, Central and North Africa, Iraq, the Czech republic, Hungary, Greece, northwestern Europe, and the Middle East. This race of men was characterized by prominent eyebrow ridges (like modern Australian Aborigines), a low forehead, a long narrow skull, a protruding upper jaw and a strong lower jaw with a short chin. They were deep-chested, large-boned individuals with a powerful build. It should be emphasized, however, that none of these features fall outside the range of normal human anatomy. Interestingly, the brain size (based on cranial capacity) of Neanderthal man was actually *larger* than average for that of modern man, though this is rarely emphasized.

Most of the misconceptions about Neanderthal man resulted from the claims of the Frenchman Marcelin Boule who, in 1908, studied two Neanderthal skeletons that were found in France (LeMoustier and La Chapelle-aux-Saints). Boule declared Neanderthal men to be anatomically and intellectually inferior brutes who were more closely related to apes than humans. He asserted that they had a slumped posture, a "monkey-like" arrangement of certain spinal vertebrae and even claimed that their feet were of a "grasping type" (like those of gorillas and chimpanzees). Boule concluded that Neanderthal man could not have walked erectly, but rather must have walked in a clumsy fashion. These highly biased and inaccurate views prevailed and were even expanded by many other evolutionists up to the mid-1950s.

In 1957, the anatomists William Straus and A. J. Cave examined one of the French Neanderthals (La Chapelle-aux-Saints) and determined that the individual suffered from severe arthritis (as suggested by Virchow nearly 100 years earlier), which had affected the vertebrae and bent the posture. The jaw also had been affected.

These observations are consistent with the Ice Age climate in which Neanderthals had lived. They may well have sought shelter in caves and this, together with poor diet and lack of sunlight, could easily have lead to diseases that affect the bones, such as rickets.

In addition to anatomical evidence, there is a growing body of cultural evidence for the fully human status of Neanderthals. They buried their dead and had elaborate funeral customs that included arranging the body and covering it with flowers. They made a variety of stone tools and worked with skins and leather. A wood flute was recently discovered among Neanderthal remains. There is even evidence that suggests that he engaged in medical care. Some Neanderthal specimens show evidence of survival to old age despite numerous wounds, broken bones, blindness and disease. This suggests that these individuals were cared for and nurtured by others who showed human compassion.

Still, efforts continue to be made to somehow dehumanize Neanderthal man. Many evolutionists now even insist that Neanderthal man is not even directly related to modern man because of some differences in a small fragment of DNA! There is, in fact, nothing about Neanderthals that is in any way inferior to modern man. One of the world's foremost authorities on Neanderthal man, Erik Trinkaus, concludes: "Detailed comparisons of Neanderthal skeletal remains with those of modern humans have shown that there is nothing in Neanderthal anatomy that conclusively indicates locomotor, manipulative, intellectual or linguistic abilities inferior to those of modern humans."[3]

Conclusion

Why then are there continued efforts to make apes out of man and man out of apes? In one of the most remarkably frank and candid assessments of the whole subject and methodology of paleoanthropology, Dr. David Pilbeam (a distinguished professor of anthropology) suggested the following:

Perhaps generations of students of human evolution, including myself, have been flailing about in the dark; that our data base is too sparse, too slippery, for it to be able to mold our theories. Rather the theories are more statements about us and ideology than about the past. Paleoanthropology reveals more about how humans view themselves than it does about how humans came about. But that is heresy.[4]

Oh, that these heretical words were printed as a warning on every textbook, magazine, newspaper article and statue that presumes to deal with the bestial origin of man!

No, we are not descended from apes. Rather, God created man as the crown of His creation on Day Six. We are a special creation of God, made in His image, to bring Him glory. What a revolution this truth would make, if our evolutionized culture truly understood it!

1.   S. Zuckerman, *Beyond the Ivory Tower* (New York: Taplinger Pub. Co., 1970), p. 64.

2.   *American Journal of Physical Anthropology* 60 (1983): 279–317.

3.   *Natural History* 87 (1978): 10.

4.   *American Scientist* 66 (1978): 379.

 **David Menton** received his PhD in Cell Biology from Brown University. Now retired, Dr. Menton served as a biomedical research technician at Mayo Clinic and then as an associate professor of anatomy at Washington University School of Medicine (St. Louis) for more than 30 years. He was a consulting editor in histology for Stedman's Medical Dictionary, and has received numerous awards for his teaching. Dr. Menton is a popular speaker for Answers in Genesis and has spoken throughout the US and Canada on the creation/evolution issue for nearly twenty years.

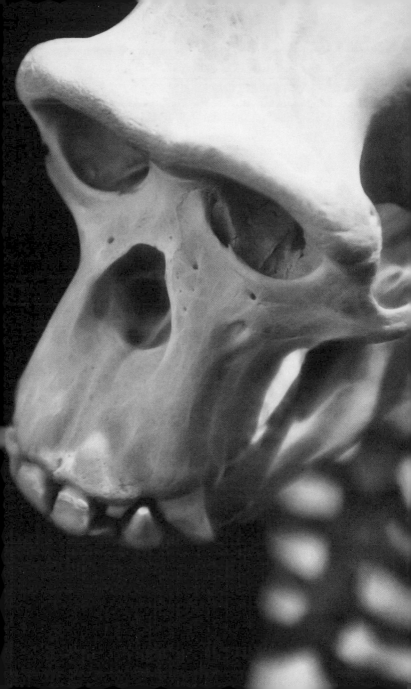

Hasn't Evolution Been Proven True?

by A. J. Monty White

Anyone who has read Genesis 1–11 realizes that the modern teachings of molecules-to-man evolution are at odds with what God says. So what is the response to evolution from a biblical and scientific perspective? Let's take a closer look.

Evolutionists often say that *evolution* simply means "change." However, in reality it means a certain kind of change. The word is now accepted to mean the change of nonliving chemicals into simple life-forms into more complex life-forms and finally into humans—what might be called *from-goo-to-you-via-the-zoo*. We are informed that this change occurred over millions of years, and the dominant mechanism that is supposed to have driven it is natural selection coupled with mutations.

Furthermore, the word *evolution* has also been applied to non-living things. Almost everything is said to have evolved—the solar system, stars, the universe, as well as social and legal systems. Everything is said to be the product of evolution. However, the three major forms of evolution are

1. Stellar evolution
2. Chemical evolution
3. Biological evolution.

The story of evolution leaves no room for a supernatural Creator. Evolutionary processes are supposed to be purely naturalistic. This means that even the need for a supernatural Creator disappears because it is argued that the natural world can create new and better or more complex creatures by itself. The implication of this is very revealing: evolution means "no God" and if there is no God, then there are no rules—no commandments, no God-given rules which we must obey. We can therefore live our lives as we please, for according to evolutionary philosophy, there is no God to whom we have to give an account. No wonder molecules-to-man evolution is attractive to so many, for it allows them to live as they please. This is called relative morality.

Does the Bible teach evolution?

The simple answer to this question is "No." In Genesis 1 we read the account of the creation (not the evolution) of everything—the universe, the sun, moon, and stars, the planet earth with all its varied plant and animal kinds, including the pinnacle of God's creation—humans. Nowhere in this account do we read about molecules-to-man evolution. Furthermore, there was no time for evolution, for God supernaturally created everything in six literal days (Exodus 20:11, 31:17).

There are those who argue that Genesis 1 is a simplified account of evolution. But such a hypothesis does not stand up to scrutiny. A quick look at the order of the events in Genesis 1 and in evolution shows this (see chart below[1]). The order of events is quite different, and the Genesis account of creation bears no relation to the evolutionary account of origins.

Evolution	Genesis
Sun before earth	Earth before sun
Dry land before sea	Sea before dry land
Atmosphere before sea	Sea before atmosphere
Sun before light on earth	Light on earth before sun
Stars before earth	Earth before stars
Earth at same time as planets	Earth before other planets

Evolution	Genesis
Sea creatures before land plants	Land plants before sea creatures
Earthworms before starfish	Starfish before earthworms
Land animals before trees	Trees before land animals
Death before man	Man before death
Thorns and thistles before man	Man before thorns and thistles
TB pathogens & cancer before man (dinosaurs had TB and cancer)	Man before TB pathogens and cancer
Reptiles before birds	Birds before reptiles
Land mammals before whales	Whales before land animals
Land mammals before bats	Bats before land animals
Dinosaurs before birds	Birds before dinosaurs
Insects before flowering plants	Flowering plants before insects
Sun before plants	Plants before sun
Dinosaurs before dolphins	Dolphins before dinosaurs
Land reptiles before pterosaurs	Pterosaurs before land reptiles

In spite of this, some argue that there is a major difference between "make" and "create" (the Hebrew words are *asah* and *bara*, respectively). They argue that God *created* some things—for example, the heaven and the earth as recorded in Genesis 1:1 and the marine and flying creatures as recorded in Genesis 1:21. They then argue that God *made* other things, perhaps by evolution from pre-existing materials—for example, the sun, moon, and stars as recorded in Genesis 1:16, and the beasts and cattle as recorded in Genesis 1:25. Though these words have slightly different nuances of meaning, they are often used interchangeably, as seen clearly where *asah* (to make) and *bara* (to create) are used in reference to the same act (the creation of man, Genesis 1:26–27). Nothing in Genesis 1 leads to the conclusion that God used evolutionary processes to produce His creation.

There is a further problem with believing that the Genesis account of creation should be interpreted as an evolutionary account. One of the things that drives evolution is *death*. Yet the Bible teaches quite clearly that death was introduced into the perfect world as a result of Adam's sin. Neither human nor animal death existed until this event—both humans and animals were originally vegetarian (Genesis 1:29–30 shows that plants are not living creatures, as land and sea creatures, birds, and people are). The original world that God created was death-free, and so evolution could not have occurred before humans were created.

Stellar evolution: the big bang

The big bang is the most prominent naturalistic view of the origin of the universe in the same way that neo-Darwinian evolution is the naturalistic view of living systems. The difference between what the Bible teaches about the origin of the universe and what the evolutionists teach can be summed up as follows: the Bible teaches that "in the beginning God created" and the evolutionists teach, in essence, that "in the beginning nothing became something and exploded."

According to the big bang, our universe is supposed to have suddenly popped into existence and rapidly expanded and given rise to the countless billions of galaxies with their countless billions of stars.

In support of the idea that nothing can give rise to the universe, cosmologists argue that quantum mechanics predicts that a vacuum can, under some circumstances, give rise to matter. But the problem with this line of reasoning is that a vacuum is *not* nothing; it is something—it is a vacuum that can be made to appear or disappear, as in the case of the Torricellian vacuum, which is found at the sealed end of a mercury barometer. All logic predicts that if you have nothing, nothing will happen. It is against all known logic and all laws of science to believe that the universe is the product of nothing. This concept is similar to hoping that an empty bank account will suddenly give rise to billions of dollars all on its own.

However, if we accept that the universe and everything in it came from nothing (and also from *nowhere*) then we have to follow this to its logical conclusion. This means that not only is all the physical material of the universe the product of nothing, but also other things. For example, we are forced to accept that nothing (which has no mind, no morals, and no conscience) created reason and logic; understanding and comprehension; complex ethical codes and legal systems; a sense of right and wrong; art, music, drama, comedy, literature, and dance; and belief systems that include God. These are just a few of the philosophical implications of the big bang hypothesis.

Chemical evolution: the origin of life

It is commonly believed (because it is taught in our schools and colleges) that laboratory experiments have proved conclusively that living organisms evolved from nonliving chemicals. Many people believe that life has been created in the laboratory by scientists who study chemical evolution.

The famous experiment conducted by Stanley Miller in 1953 is often quoted as proof of this. Yet the results of such experiments show nothing of the sort. These experiments, designed as they are by intelligent humans, show that under certain conditions, certain organic compounds can be formed from inorganic compounds.

In fact, what the *intelligent* scientists are actually saying is, "If I can just synthesize life in the laboratory, then I will have proven that no *intelligence* was necessary to form life in the beginning." Their experiments are simply trying to prove the opposite—that an intelligence is required to create life.

If we look carefully at Miller's experiment, we will see that what he did fails to address the evolution of life. He took a mixture of gases (ammonia, hydrogen, methane, and water vapor) and he passed an electric current through them. He did this in order to reproduce the effect of lightning passing through a mixture of gases that he thought might have composed the earth's atmosphere millions of years ago. As a result, he produced a mixture of amino acids. Because amino acids are the building blocks of proteins and proteins are considered to be the building blocks of living systems, Miller's experiment was hailed as proof that life had evolved by chance on the earth millions of years ago.

There are a number of objections to such a conclusion.

1. There is no proof that the earth ever had an atmosphere composed of the gases used by Miller in his experiment.

2. The next problem is that in Miller's experiment he was careful to make sure there was no oxygen present. If oxygen was present, then the amino acids would not form. However, if oxygen was absent from the earth, then there would be no ozone layer, and if there was no ozone layer the ultraviolet radiation would penetrate the atmosphere and would destroy the amino acids as soon as they were formed. So the dilemma facing the evolutionist can be summed up this way: amino acids would not form in an atmosphere *with* oxygen and amino acids would be destroyed in an atmosphere *without* oxygen.

3. The next problem concerns the so-called handedness of the amino acids. Because of the way that carbon atoms join up with other atoms, amino acids exist in two forms—the right-handed form and the left-handed form. Just as your right hand and left hand are identical in all respects except for their handedness, so the two forms of amino acids are identical except for their handedness. In all living systems only left-handed amino acids are found. Yet Miller's experiment produced a mixture of right-handed and left-handed amino acids in identical proportions. As only the left-handed ones are used in living systems, this mixture is useless for the evolution of living systems.

4. Another major problem for the chemical evolutionist is the origin of the information that is found in living systems. There

are various claims about the amount of information that is found in the human genome, but it can be conservatively estimated as being equivalent to a few thousand books, each several hundred pages long. Where did this information come from? Chance does not generate information. This observation caused the late Professor Sir Fred Hoyle and his colleague, Professor Chandra Wickramasinghe of Cardiff University, to conclude that the evolutionist is asking us to believe that a tornado can pass through a junk yard and assemble a jumbo jet.

The problems outlined above show that, far from creating life in the laboratory, the chemical evolutionists have not shown that living systems arose by chance from nonliving chemicals. Furthermore, the vast amount of information contained in the nucleus of a living cell shows that living systems could not have evolved from nonliving chemicals. The only explanation for the existence of living systems is that they must have been created.

Biological evolution: common descent?

Comparative anatomy is the name given to the science that deals with the structure of animals. Comparing the anatomy of one kind of animal with another is supposed to prove descent from a common ancestor. This is often put forward as strong evidence for evolution. However, the science of comparative anatomy can just as easily be used as evidence of creation, as we shall see.

The bones of a horse are different from our bones, but there is such a similarity that if we are familiar with the human skeleton, we could easily identify and name the bones of a horse. We could do the same if we studied the skeleton of a salamander, a crocodile, a bird, or a bat. However, not only are the bones similar, but so also are other anatomical structures, such as muscles, the heart, the liver, the kidneys, the eyes, the lungs, the digestive tract, and so on. This is interpreted by the evolutionists as proof that these various animals are all descended from a common ancestor.

One of the classic examples that is often used in biology textbooks to illustrate comparative anatomy is the forelimbs of amphibians, reptiles, humans, birds, bats, and quadrupeds. In the illustration, it can be seen that all the forelimbs of these six different types of creatures have an upper arm bone (the humerus) and two lower arm bones (the radius and the ulna), although in the case of the bat there is only one bone, called the radio-ulna.

Evolutionists teach that these structures are said to be homologous when they are similar in structure and origin, but not necessarily in function. But notice how subtly the notion of origins is introduced into the definition. The bat's wing is considered to be homologous to the forelimb of a salamander because it is similar in structure and believed to have the same origin. However, it is not considered to be homologous to the wing of an insect because, even though it has the same function, it is not considered to have the same origin. However, the fact that the two structures

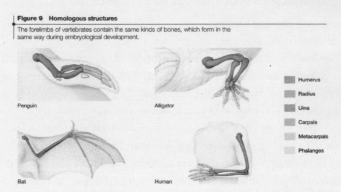

Figure 9 Homologous structures

The forelimbs of vertebrates contain the same kinds of bones, which form in the same way during embryological development.

Penguin

Alligator

Bat

Human

- Humerus
- Radius
- Ulna
- Carpals
- Metacarpals
- Phalanges

The presence of homologous structures can actually be interpreted as evidence for a common designer. Contrary to the oversimplified claim in this figure, the forelimbs of vertebrates do not form in the same way. Specifically, in frogs the phalanges form as buds that grow outward and in humans they form from a ridge that develops furrows inward. The fact that the bones can be correlated does not mean that they are evidence of a single common ancestor.[2]

are similar does not necessarily mean that they are derived from a common ancestor.

We have to realize that the entire line of reasoning by evolutionists is based upon a single assumption: that the degree of similarity between organisms indicates the degree of supposed relationship of the said organisms. In other words, it is argued that if animals look alike, then they must be closely related (from an evolutionary point of view), and if they do not look very much alike, then they are more distantly related. But this is just an assumption.

In fact, there is another logical reason why things look alike—creation by an intelligent designer using a common blueprint. This is the reason that Toyota and Ford motor vehicles look so much alike. They are built to a common plan—you only have to look at them to realize this. However, the problem with the living world is that in many cases either explanation (i.e., evolution or creation) appears to be logical and it is often impossible for us to tell which is the more reasonable explanation. This is why it is important for us to understand which worldview we are using to interpret the evidence.

There is, however, one discovery that appears to make the evolutionary view of descent from a common ancestor look illogical and flawed. This discovery is that structures that appear homologous often develop under the control of genes that are *not* homologous. If the structures evolved from the same source, you would expect the same genes to make the structures. The fact that these structures are similar (or homologous) is apparent, but the reason is not because of Darwinian evolution. It is more logical and reasonable to believe in a common Creator rather than a common ancestor.

Many evolutionists readily admit that they have failed to find evidence of the evolution of large structures such as bones and muscles, so instead they argue that they have found homology among the complex organic molecules that are found in living systems. One of these is hemoglobin, the protein that carries oxygen in red blood cells. Although this protein is found in nearly all vertebrates, it is also found in some invertebrates (worms, starfish, clams, and insects) and also in some bacteria. Yet there is no evidence of the evolution of this chemical—in all cases, the same kind of molecule is complete and fully functional. If evolution has occurred, it should be possible to map out how hemoglobin evolved, but this cannot be done. To the creationist, however, hemoglobin crops up complete and fully functional wherever the Creator deems it fitting in His plan.

Missing links

Our English word *fossil* is from the Latin *fossilis*, which means "something dug up." The present-day meaning of the word fossil is a relic or trace of past life preserved in the rocks. This can be a preserved hard part of the plant or animal, such as a stem or a leaf or a shell or a bone or a tooth; it can also be a soft part such as skin or even excrement (called *coprolites*), or it can be a trace made by the creature when it was alive, such as a footprint. All the fossils that are found in all the sedimentary rocks are regarded together as the fossil record.

Charles Darwin proposed the gradual evolution of life-forms over a long period of time. If this has happened, you would expect to find this gradual evolution of one kind of life-form into another kind to be recorded in the fossil record. However, this evolutionary account of one kind of life-form changing into another kind is *not* recorded in the fossils. There are many instances where variations within a kind are found (for example, different varieties of elephant or dinosaur) but there are no examples of in-between kinds. Both evolutionists and creationists agree that the intermediate transitional forms expected on the basis of slow gradual change of one kind of creature into another kind is not found fossilized in the sedimentary rocks. In other words, the transitional forms are missing—hence the term "missing links."

Charles Darwin himself realized that his theory was not supported by the fossil record, for he wrote in his *Origin of Species*:

> The number of intermediate varieties which have formerly existed on earth must be truly enormous. Why then is not every geological formation and every stratum full of such intermediate links? Geology assuredly does not reveal any such finely graduated organic chain: and this, perhaps, is the most obvious and gravest objection which can be urged against my theory.[3]

When Charles Darwin penned these words, he attributed this absence of transitional forms to what he called the "extreme imperfection" of the fossil record. Since that time, however, literally millions of fossils have been found, but still the transitional forms are absent. The fossil record does not show the continuous development of one kind of creature into another, but it shows different kinds of creatures that are fully functional with no ancestors or descendants which are different kinds of creatures.

It cannot be overemphasized that there are many places in the fossil record where it is expected that plenty of intermediate forms should be found—yet they are not there. All the evolutionists ever point to is a handful of highly debatable transitional forms (e.g., horses), whereas they should be able to show us thousands of incontestable examples. This is very noticeable when looking at the fossil record of some of the more peculiar kinds of animals such as the *cetacean* (whales, dolphins, and porpoises), the *sirenia* (manatees, dugongs, and sea cows), the *pinnipedia* (sea lions, seals, and walruses), kangaroos, bats, dragonflies, and spiders. Their supposed evolutionary origins and descent are represented by missing links and speculations rather than factual evidence.

Even alleged transitional forms in supposed human evolution fall short. In fact, most so-called missing links fall into three categories: extinct ape, living ape, or human. The following chart gives some of the most common scientific names and their classifications.

Name	What is it?*
Australopithecus afarensis, such as "Lucy"	Extinct ape
Australopithecus africanus	Extinct ape
Australopithecus boisei	Extinct ape
Australopithecus robustus	Extinct ape
Pan troglodytes and *Pan paniscus* (chimpanzee)	Living ape
Gorilla gorilla and *Gorilla beringei* (gorilla)	Living ape
Pongo pygmaeus and *Pongo abelii* (orangutan)	Living ape
Ramapithecus	Extinct ape (extinct orangutan)
Homo habilis	Junk category mixing some human and some ape fossils
Homo floresiensis	Human (dwarf, pygmy)**
Homo ergaster	Human
Homo erectus, such as "Peking man" and "Java man"	Human***
Homo neanderthalensis (Neanderthals)	Human
Homo heidelbergensis	Human
Homo sapiens (modern & archaic)	Human

* An accurate classification of these kinds of fossils depends on an accurate starting point. Some fossils have been misclassified. The ones labeled as humans (*Homo heidelbergensis*, *Homo erectus*, etc.), indeed show variation, but they are still human. This is also true of the different ape kinds. Variation, not evolution, is what we would expect from the clear teachings of the Bible.

** Not everyone agrees that *Homo floresiensis* was a dwarf or pygmy; the jury is still out.

*** For the most part these two classifications are anatomically human. However, a number of finds that are not human but rather apelike have been included as part of the **Homo erectus** category, due to evolutionary beliefs. These apelike finds should be reclassified.

It is obvious that the evolutionists have "faith" in the original existence of the missing transitional forms.

Evolution of new kinds?

Charles Darwin visited the Galápagos Islands and brought back samples of the different finches that lived on the different islands. He observed that they had different shaped beaks, which appeared to suit the type of food that the finches ate. From this observation, Darwin concluded that a pair or flock of finches had flown to these islands at some time in the past and that the different beaks on the finches had evolved via natural selection, depending on what island they lived on and consequently what they fed on. From these types of simple observations and conclusions, Darwin developed not only the idea of the evolution of species but also the idea of chemicals-to-chemist evolution!

But let us consider exactly what Darwin actually observed—finches living on different islands feeding on different types of food having different beaks. What did he propose? That these finches had descended from a pair or flock of finches. In other words, he proposed that finches begat finches—that is, they reproduced after their own kind. This is exactly what the Bible teaches in Genesis 1.

It cannot be overemphasized that no one has ever seen one kind of plant or animal changing into another different kind. Darwin did not observe this, even though he proposed that it does happen. There are literally thousands of plant and animal kinds on the earth today, and these verify what the Bible indicates in Genesis 1 about plants and animals reproducing after their own kind.

Plants and animals reproducing after their own kind is what we observe, and it is what Charles Darwin observed in finches on the Galápagos Islands. For example, we see different varieties of *Brassica*—kale, cabbage, cauliflower are all varieties of the wild common mustard *Brassica oleracea*. Furthermore, another perfect example of a kind is the hundreds of different varieties of dogs, including spaniels, terriers, bulldogs, Chihuahuas, Great Danes, German shepherds, Irish wolfhounds, and greyhounds, which are all capable of interbreeding, together with wolves, jackals, dingoes, and coyotes. All are descended from the two representatives of the dog kind that came off Noah's Ark.

Conclusion

We have seen that the Bible does not teach evolution. There is no demonstrable evidence for the big bang, and chemical evolution has failed miserably in spite of evolutionists' attempts to create living systems in the laboratory. Similarities in the structure found in living systems can be interpreted better as evidence for a common design rather than a common ancestry. In spite of billions of fossils being found, there are no unquestionable fossils that show a transition between any of the major life-forms.

Natural selection (done in the wild) and artificial selection (as done by breeders) produce enormous varieties *within* the different kinds of plants and animals. It has proved an impossible feat, however, to change one kind of creature into a different kind of plant or animal. The so-called "kind barrier" has never been crossed. Such evolution has never been observed. This has been pointed out by none other than evolutionary Professor Richard Dawkins, who confidently asserted in an interview that evolution has been observed but then added, "It's just that it hasn't been observed while it's happening."[4]

1. Terry Mortenson, "Evolution vs. creation: the order of events matters!" Answers in Genesis, http://www.answersingenesis.org/docs2006/0404order.asp.

2. G. Johnson and P. Raven, *Biology* (Austin, TX: Holt, Rinehart, and Winston, 2006), p. 286.

3. Charles Darwin, *The Origin of Species* (London: Penguin Books, 1968), p. 291.

4. Richard Dawkins, interview by Bill Moyers, *NOW*, PBS, December 3, 2004, http://www.pbs.org/now/transcript/transcript349_full.html#dawkins.

Monty White holds a BS with honors, a PhD in the field of gas kinetics from the University College of Wales, Aberystwyth, and has completed a two-year post-doctoral fellowship at the same University. Dr. White subsequently served in a number of university administrative posts. Over the years he has written several books and numerous articles relating to creation-evolution, and science and the Bible, as well as making several appearances on British television and radio programs dealing with these issues.

The Ghost of Darwin

by Ken Ham

I "I don't believe in ghosts! But the ghost of Darwin is a very real phenomenon nonetheless."

On February 12, 1809, in the modest town of Shrewsbury, England, Susannah Darwin gave birth to her now-famous son Charles in their family home called The Mount.

Darwin's presence where he was born

That was roughly 200 years ago, yet as you walk through the town of Shrewsbury, you sense Darwin's influence (his "ghost") all around. Darwin Street, Darwin Terrace, Darwin House, Darwin Gardens, and the Darwin Shopping Center are just a few of the landmarks that honor and immortalize this man.

Before patrons enter the town library, they are greeted by a statue of an older Darwin and a plaque, which informs them that this is the very building where Darwin received his education.

As area students enter their modern school, they see a prominent statue of a young Darwin, with sculptures of various animals he saw on the Galápagos Islands, which he used to support his idea of natural selection.

Darwin's ghost also inhabits the classrooms of this school. There students are taught that Darwinian evolution is indisputable fact—the same fact that is taught in secular schools around the world.

Shrewsbury also had major celebrations in 2009, the 200th

anniversary of Darwin's birth and the 150th anniversary of the publication of his famous work *On the Origin of Species by Means of Natural Selection, or the Preservation of Favoured Races in the Struggle for Life*. However, town officials did not just gear up for 2009. With the prospect of ongoing financial development through the promotion of Darwin's roots in Shrewsbury, they commissioned a 90-page, 30-year strategic plan centered on celebrating and commercializing Darwin.[1] His ghost will become even better known and celebrated (not just in Shrewsbury, but around the world) and will be the focus for tourists visiting the area.

Isn't it ironic that Darwin—a man who popularized a philosophy destructive to the foundations of the church—was honored by the Church of England by being buried in the foundations of the building? His grave *(right)* is in the actual floor of Westminster Abbey in London, England *(left)*.

Darwin's presence in the church

The really sad aspect of all this is that Darwin's ghost has invaded the church. Hundreds of thousands of churches around the world have adopted Darwinian evolution and reinterpreted the history in Genesis to fit with Darwin's anti-Christian beliefs. Theistic evolution (the belief that God used evolution) has become a dominant position in much of the church in England and has spread from there around the world.

In 2006, hundreds of churches in the USA signed up to celebrate what they called Evolution Sunday to honor Darwin on the anniversary of his 197th birthday.[2] The clergy of these churches took this time to teach that evolution and the Bible are compatible. Evolution Sunday promoted the compromised views of churches that reject the clear, literal interpretation of Genesis and, instead, add in the evolutionary ideas of an unbeliever. This new tradition continues today as evolution is embraced by churches across the world.

The result of Darwin's presence

As a result of such compromise, which began in a big way in the Church of England during the nineteenth century, subsequent generations in the church began rejecting more of the authority of Scripture. Observers note that whereas England's church attendance before World War II was 40–50 percent, by 2003 "only 7.5 percent of the population went to church on Sundays and that, in the past 10 years—billed by the churches as

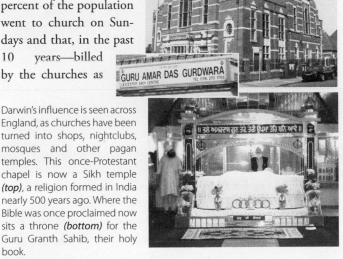

Darwin's influence is seen across England, as churches have been turned into shops, nightclubs, mosques and other pagan temples. This once-Protestant chapel is now a Sikh temple *(top)*, a religion formed in India nearly 500 years ago. Where the Bible was once proclaimed now sits a throne *(bottom)* for the Guru Granth Sahib, their holy book.

the 'Decade of Evangelism'—church attendance dropped by an alarming 22 percent."[3]

The ghost of Darwin is felt as one travels across England and sees church buildings that have been turned into shops, mosques, nightclubs, and worse.

England's education system and culture, as a whole, were once primarily built on the foundation of God's Word. The United States was also solidly founded on God's Word. However, Christians in England, America, and many other nations have allowed that once-solid foundation to be replaced by the shaky foundation of man's word, particularly Darwin's evolutionary ideas and the belief in millions of years.

Darwin's legacy—an assault against God

In 1859, from his home near the small village of Downe in England, Charles Darwin wrote *The Origin of Species*. This book popularized the idea that life could be explained by natural processes, without God. A few years later Darwin published the book *Descent of Man*, applying his evolutionary ideas to the origin of man and postulating that mankind evolved from ape-like ancestors.

From this house spread a philosophy that attacked the authority of God's Word in Genesis—the foundational history for all Christian doctrine (including the gospel), and, in fact, for the entire Bible.

This fact is clearly illustrated by a quote in the home's final exhibit, which is mounted on top of the silhouetted text of Genesis 1. It reads:

> Many Christians believed that the world and everything in it, including mankind, had been **created by God** in the beginning and had remained unaltered ever since . . . . Darwin's theory made **nonsense** of all of this. He said that the world was a constantly changing place and

Darwin's family home in Kent, England, now a museum, is where Darwin wrote his two most famous works.

that all living creatures were changing too. Far from being created in God's own image, Darwin suggested that human life had probably started out as something far more primitive—the story of **Adam and Eve was a myth** [emphasis added].

The quote above sums up the legacy of Darwin. His ghost has spread around the world, and it is totally consistent with what Darwin himself wrote in his autobiography:

I had gradually come, by this time, to see that the Old Testament from its manifestly false history of the world, with the Tower of Babel, the rainbow as a sign, etc., etc., from its attributing to God the feelings of a revengeful tyrant, was no more to be trusted than the sacred books of the Hindoos, or the beliefs of any barbarian.[4]

Conclusion

Darwinian thinking is seen in the pages of public school textbooks and in the humanistic mindset of the next generation. His ghost is present in empty church pews, in secular science, in revisionist history, in the hallowed halls of art museums, and in the signs, movies, and brochures at zoos and national parks worldwide. Christian morality has all but collapsed in Western society. The culture has been secularized, and young adults who were brought up in church, but with a naturalistic foundation, are turning away from Christianity. These are a few results of the evolutionary thinking and compromised doctrines that permeate even the church today.

Christians should pray that the Lord rebuilds the foundations of His house that shifted from the firm ground of His Word and compromised because of the works of a man.

Such rebuilding must start with the literal history of Genesis 1–11—a return to the authority of the Bible. Christians must rally together to stop Darwin's ghost from destroying the culture.

1. Darwin Birthplace Society, http://darwinbirthplace.orangeleaf.net/Darwin.pdf.

2. University of Washington Oshkosh, http://www.uwosh.edu/colleges/cols/rel_evol_sun_orig.htm.

3. "Church will be dead in 40 years' time," *The Independent*, April 16, 2000.

4. Charles Darwin, *The Autobiography of Charles Darwin, 1809–1882* (New York: Norton, 1993), p. 85.

Ken Ham is President and CEO of Answers in Genesis–USA and the Creation Museum. Ken's bachelor's degree in applied science (with an emphasis on environmental biology) was awarded by the Queensland Institute of Technology in Australia. He also holds a diploma of education from the University of Queensland. In recognition of the contribution Ken has made to the church in the USA and internationally, Ken has been awarded two honorary doctorates: a Doctor of Divinity (1997) from Temple Baptist College in Cincinnati, Ohio and a Doctor of Literature (2004) from Liberty University in Lynchburg, Virginia.

Ken has authored or co-authored many books concerning the authority and accuracy of God's Word and the effects of evolutionary thinking, including *Genesis of a Legacy* and *The Lie: Evolution*.

Since moving to America in 1987, Ken has become one of the most in-demand Christian conference speakers and talk show guests in America. He has appeared on national shows such as Fox's *The O'Reilly Factor* and *Fox and Friends in the Morning*; CNN's *The Situation Room with Wolf Blitzer*, ABC's *Good Morning America*, the BBC, *CBS News Sunday Morning*, *The NBC Nightly News with Brian Williams*, and *The PBS News Hour with Jim Lehrer*.

Darwin's Plantation

by Ken Ham

*H*e crouched in the corner of the cage. With his head between his knees and his arms pulling his legs tightly to his chest, he shielded himself as best he could from the crowd. The iron bars around him offered a certain level of physical protection from the mob that swirled around him—but they did nothing to protect him from the stares, from the laughter, from the jeers that rained down upon him day after day after day. Coins and stones pelted his flesh, the crowd hoping to instigate some sort of reaction. His infrequent backlashes of anger only incited them further.

Thousands of miles from his home and the graves of his slaughtered ancestors, he dreamed of the days when he moved freely and intently through his homeland. He longed to hunt again with his kinsman. He starved for the warm immersion of fellowship with his wife and children.

But that was all behind him now. His family and his tribe had been murdered in the name of evolution. And now he cowered in the cage, a prisoner in Darwin's plantation.

A man named "Ota"

Ota Benga was born in 1881 in Central Africa, where he grew strong and keen in the ways of the wilderness. The husband of one and the father of two, he returned one day from a successful elephant hunt to find that the camp he called "home" had ceased to exist. His wife, children, and friends lay slaughtered, their bodies mutilated in a campaign of terror by the Belgian government's thugs against "the evolutionary inferior natives." Ota was later captured, taken to a village, and sold into slavery.

He was first brought to the United States from the Belgian Congo in 1904 by the noted African explorer Samuel Verner, who had bought him at a slave auction. At 4'11" tall, weighing a mere 103 pounds, he was often referred to as "the boy." In reality, he was a son, a husband, and a father. Ota was first displayed as an "emblematic savage" in the anthropology wing of the 1904 St. Louis World's Fair. Along with other pygmies, he was studied by scientists to learn how the "barbaric races" compared with intellectually defective Caucasians on intelligence tests and how they responded to things such as pain.[1]

The July 23, 1904, *Scientific American* reported:

> They are small, ape-like, elfish creatures . . . they live in absolute savagery, and while they exhibit many ape-like features in their bodies, they possess a certain alertness which appears to make them more intelligent than other Negroes . . . the existence of the pygmies is of the rudest; they do not practice agriculture, and keep no domestic animals. They live by means of hunting and snaring, eking this out by means of thieving from the big Negroes, on the outskirts of whose tribes they usually establish their little colonies, though they are as unstable as water, and range far and wide through the forests. They have seemingly become acquainted with metal only through contact with superior beings.

They failed to mention 1902 research by H.H. Johnston in the *Smithsonian Report* that found the pygmies to be a very talented group. When studied in their natural environment, Johnston found that they were experts at mimicry, and they were physically agile, quick, and nimble. They were exceptional hunters, with highly developed social skills and structure. While outsiders considered them primitive, the pygmies actually held strong monotheistic beliefs about God. More recent research has confirmed, "The religion of the Ituri Forest Pygmies is founded on the belief that God possesses the totality of vital force, of which he distributes part to his creatures, an act by which he brings them into existence or perfects them. . . . According to a favorite pygmies saying, 'He who made the light also makes the darkness.'"[2] When Verner had visited their African king, "He was met with songs and presents, food and palm wine, drums. He was carried in a hammock."

But the Darwinists failed to take note of any of these things. Such observations didn't fit their preconceived notions of evolution or their view that the pygmies were inferior, sub-human beings. When the pygmies were in St. Louis, they were greeted with laughter, staring, poking, and prodding. "People came to take their picture and run away . . . some came to fight with them. . . . Verner had contracted to bring pygmies safely back to Africa. It was often a struggle just to keep them from being torn to pieces at the fair. Repeatedly . . . the crowds became agitated and ugly; pushing and grabbing in a frenzied quality. Each time Ota and the Batwa were extracted only with difficulty."[3]

The exhibit was said to be "exhaustively scientific" in its demonstration of the stages of human evolution. Therefore, they required the darkest blacks to be clearly distinguished from the dominant whites. Ota's presence as a member of "the lowest known culture" was meant to be a graphic contrast with the Caucasians, who represented humanity's "highest culmination."

Meanwhile, the anthropologists in charge of the display continued their research by testing and measuring. In one case "the primitive's head was severed from the body and boiled down to the skull." Believing that skull size was an index of intelligence, the scientists were amazed to discover that the "primitive" skull was larger than that which belonged to the statesman Daniel Webster.[4]

After the fair, Verner took Ota and the other pygmies back to Africa. Ota soon remarried, but his second spouse died from a poisonous snakebite. He was also ostracized from his own people because of his association with the white people. Back in his homeland, Ota had found himself entirely alone. He returned to America with Verner, who said he would return him to Africa on his next trip. It was not to be. Once back in America, Verner tried to sell his animals to zoos and sell the crates of artifacts that he brought back from Africa. Verner was also having serious money problems and could not afford to take care of Ota.

When Verner presented Ota to Dr. Hornady, the director of the Bronx Zoological Gardens, it was clear that he would again go on display—but this time, the display took on an even more sinister twist. On September 9, 1906, *The New York Times* headline screamed, "Bushman shares a cage with Bronx Park apes." Although Dr. Hornady insisted that he was merely offering an "intriguing exhibit" for the public, the *Times* reported that Dr. Hornady "apparently saw no difference between a wild beast and the little black man; and for the first time in any American zoo, a human being was being displayed in a cage."

On September 10, the *Times* reported:

> There was always a crowd before the cage, most of the time roaring with laughter, and from almost every corner of the garden could be heard the question "Where is the pygmy?" The answer was, "In the monkey house."

Bradford and Blume, who extensively researched Ota's life for the book *Ota Benga: The Pygmy in the Zoo*, noted:

> The implications of the exhibit were also clear from the visitor's questions. Was he a man or a monkey? Was he something in between? "Ist das ein Mensch?" asked a German spectator. "Is it a man?" . . . No one really mis- took apes or parrots for human beings. This "it" came so much

closer. Was it a man? Was it a monkey? Was it a forgotten stage of evolution?

Dr. Hornady was a staunch believer in Darwin's theory. *The New York Times* on September 11, 1906, reported that he had concluded that there was "a close analogy of the African savage to the apes" and that he "maintained a hierarchical view of the races."

The display was extremely successful. On September 16, 40,000 visitors came to the zoo. The crowds were so enormous that a police officer was assigned to guard Ota full time because he was "always in danger of being grabbed, yanked, poked, and pulled to pieces by the mob."[5]

Not all condoned the frenzy. A group of concerned black ministers went to Ota's defense. The September 10 *Times* reported Reverend Gordon saying, "Our race . . . is depressed enough without exhibiting one of us with the apes." On September 12, however, the *Times* retorted by saying, "The reverend colored brother should be told that evolution . . . is now taught in the textbooks of all the schools, and that it is no more debatable than the multiplication table."

The media frenzy eventually led to Ota being released from the cage, but the spectacle continued. The *Times* reported on September 18, "There were 40,000 visitors to the park on Sunday. Nearly every man, woman, and child of this crowd made for the monkey house to see the star attraction in the park—a wild man from Africa. They chased him about the grounds all day, howling, cheering, and yelling. Some of them poked him in the ribs, others tripped him up, all laughed at him."

Eventually, Hornady himself was worn down (either by the media pressure or by the exhaustion that the spectacle had created). Ota was released from the zoo. In the following months, he found care at a succession of institutions and with several sympathetic individuals. In 1910, he arrived at a black community in Lynchburg, Virginia, where he found companionship and care.

He became a baptized Christian, and his English vocabulary rapidly improved. He regularly cared for the children, protecting them and teaching them to hunt. He also learned how to read and occasionally attended classes at a Lynchburg seminary. Later he was employed as a tobacco factory worker.

But Ota grew increasingly depressed, hostile, irrational, and forlorn. When people spoke to him, they noticed that he had tears in his eyes when he told them he wanted to go home. Concluding that he would never be able to return to his native land, on March 20, 1916, Ota pressed a revolver to his chest and sent a bullet through his heart.

The seeds of racism

The theory of Darwinian evolution claims that human beings changed "from-molecules-to-man" over millions and millions of years, with one of our intermediate states being that of the apes. This theory logically implies that certain "races" are more ape-like than they might be human. Ever since the theory of evolution became popular and widespread, Darwinian scientists have been attempting to form continuums that represent the evolution of humanity, with some "races" being placed closer to the apes, while others are placed higher on the evolutionary scale. These continuums are formed solely by outward appearances and are still used today to justify racism—even though modern genetics has clearly proven that our differences, few as they might be, are no deeper than the skin.

On the last page of his book, *The Descent of Man*, Charles Darwin expressed the opinion that he would rather be descended from a monkey than from a "Savage." In describing those with darker skin, he often used words like "savage," "low," and "degraded" to describe American Indians, pygmies, and almost every ethnic group whose physical appearance and culture differed from his own. In his work, pygmies have been compared to "lower organisms" and were labeled "the low integrated inhabitants of the Andaman Islands."[6]

Although racism did not begin with Darwinism, Darwin did more than any person to popularize it. After Darwin "proved" that all humans descended from apes, it was natural to conclude that some races had descended further than others. In his opinion, some races (namely the white ones) have left the others far behind, while other races (pygmies especially) have hardly matured at all. The subtitle of Darwin's classic 1859 book, *The Origin of the Species*, was *The Preservation of Favoured Races in the Struggle for Life*. The book dealt with the evolution of animals in general, and his later book, *The Descent of Man*, applied his theory to humans.

As the seeds of Darwinism continued to spread in the 1900s, the question being asked was "Who is human and what is not?" The answers were often influenced by the current interpretations of Darwinism.[7] The widely held view was that blacks evolved from the strong but less intelligent gorillas, the Orientals evolved from the orangutan, and whites evolved from the most intelligent of all primates, the chimpanzees.[8] Across the globe, such conclusions were used to justify racism, oppression, and genocide.

Within decades, however, evolution would be used as justification for the whites of Europe to turn upon themselves. The fruits of Darwinian evolution, from the Nazi conception of racial superiority to its utilization in developing their governmental policy, are well documented. The works of J. Bergman in *Perspectives on Science and the Christian Faith,* June 1992, and March 1993, are just a few examples of vast amounts of material that show the connection between evolutionary thinking and Hitler's genocidal slaughter of innocent human beings.

Jim Fletcher recalls these vivid impressions from visiting the Holocaust Museum in Washington, D.C.:

> The railroad car, once you realize what it represents, forces you in, although not in the same way that people

it memorializes were forced off aboard so many decades ago. The odd smell—which many visitors say must be the smell of death—can't be scrubbed away. It shouldn't be, for it reminds our senses in a visceral way of what happens when men leave God, and malevolent ideas go unchallenged. . . . When Adolph Hitler looked for a "final solution" for what he called the "Jewish problem"—the fact of the Jews' existence—he had only to recall what scientists like Ernest Haeckel and liberal theologians embraced: that a purposeless process, known as evolution, had generated all of life's complexity, including civilization itself. It had done so through a pitiless procedure of the strong eliminating the weak. As the influence of this idea spread, the Bible was increasingly taught as myth.[9]

Continued racism on European soil has resulted in bitter struggles and untold bloodshed between those of different "races" who occupy the same lands. The recent ethnic conflict between the Serbs and Croats snf the dissolution of Czechoslovakia into the Czech Republic and Slovakia are just a few examples.

The effect of Darwinism on racism, however, is certainly not limited to Europe. The fruit of Darwin's plantation was (and is) being reaped in my homeland of Australia, which was involved in a gruesome trade in "missing link" specimens fueled by early evolutionary and racist ideas. Documented evidence shows that the remains of perhaps 10,000 or more of Australia's Aborigines were shipped to British museums in a frenzied attempt to prove the widespread belief that they were the "missing link." Evolutionists in the United States were also strongly involved in this flourishing industry of gathering species of "sub-humans." (The Smithsonian Institution in Washington holds the remains of over 15,000 individuals!) Along with museum curators from around the world, some of the top names in British science were involved in this large-scale grave robbing trade. These included anatomist

Sir Richard Cohen, anthropologist Sir Arthur Keith, and Charles Darwin himself. Darwin wrote asking for Tasmanian skulls when only four of the island's Aborigines were left alive, provided that the request not "upset" their feelings.

Some museums were not only interested in bones but also in fresh skins. These were sometimes used to provide interesting evolutionary displays when they were stuffed.[10] Good prices were being offered for such "specimens." Written evidence shows that many of the "fresh" specimens were obtained by simply going out and murdering the aboriginal people in my country. An 1866 deathbed memoir from Korah Wills, mayor of Bowen, in Queensland, Australia, graphically describes how he killed and dismembered local tribesmen in 1865 to provide a scientific specimen.

Edward Ramsay, curator of the Australian Museum in Sydney for 20 years starting in 1874, was particularly heavily involved. He published a booklet for the museum that gave instructions not only on how to rob graves, but also on how to plug bullet wounds from freshly killed "specimens." Many freelance collectors worked under his guidance. For example, four weeks after Ramsay had requested skulls of Bungee Blacks, a keen young scientist sent him two of them, announcing, "The last of their tribe, had just been shot."[11]

The seeds from Darwin's plantation even spread as far as Asia, where evolutionary thinking was used to justify their acts of racism and genocide. In order to justify their nation's expansionist aggression, the Japanese had been told that they were the most "highly evolved" race on earth. After all, the Europeans, with their longer arms and hairy chests, were clearly closer to the ape, weren't they? Westerners returned in kind, of course, often portraying the Japanese as uncivilized savages in order to dehumanize their killing with weapons of mass destruction.

In North America, Darwinism was used to justify colonial slavery as well as the elimination of "savage native tribes" who hindered the European's westward expansion in the name "manifest destiny." People on various continents wanted to "prove" that their "race" originated first. As a result, the Germans trumpeted Neanderthal fossils, the British did the same with Piltdown Man, and so on. Currently, members of the Ku Klux Klan justify their racism on the basis that they are a more evolutionary advanced race. The current Christian Identity Movement believes that Jews and blacks are not really human at all.

Today, Darwinism and evolutionary thinking also enable ordinary, respectable professionals—otherwise dedicated to the saving of life—to justify their involvement in the slaughter of millions of unborn human beings, who (like the Aborigines of earlier Darwinian thinking) are also deemed "not yet fully human."

How did we get here?

Six thousand years ago, God created a perfect world and fashioned the first two humans in His image. Humans were created to rule under God and to care for all of God's creation. After the Flood, God restated this plan to Noah and his three sons.

According to God's Word, all the people on earth today descended from Noah's three sons, who descended from the first man, Adam. So we all share the same bloodline. We're all brothers and sisters, siblings and cousins in the same family.

- We're all created by God. God formed man of dust from the ground (Genesis 2:7).

- We're all in God's image. God said, "Let Us make man in Our image" (Genesis 1:26).

- We're all one family. He [God] has made from one blood every nation (Acts 17:26).

- We're all loved by God. God so loved the world that He gave His only begotten Son (John 3:16).

While Darwinian evolution has often been used to justify genocide and racism, God's Word clearly condemns the abuse of others. God said to Noah and his sons, "But you shall not eat flesh with its life, that is, its blood. . . . from the hand of every man's brother I will require the life of man. Whoever sheds man's blood, by man his blood shall be shed, for in the image of God He made man" (Genesis 9:4–6).

God's Word condemns a long list of abuses: the abuse of the unborn, the abuse of the young, the abuse of the old, the sick, and the poor. Principles derived from God's Word also condemn discrimination based on language, culture, gender, or skin tone.

God's Word says that all people after the Flood descended from Noah's three sons. "These three were the sons of Noah, and from these the whole earth was populated" (Genesis 9:19). At Babel, mankind rebelled against God and refused to follow His Word. They lifted themselves up as the ultimate authority and began a cycle of abuse that has been repeated by every people in every generation. Later, the events of the Tower of Babel split up the human gene pool. Different combinations of genes in different groups resulted in some people having predominately light skin, some having predominately dark skin, and others with every shade in between.

With our current understanding of genetics, we now know that these biological differences are superficial and insignificant. Our physical differences are merely the result of different combinations of physical features that God put in the human gene pool at creation. Because of the small genetic differences involved, the appearance of different people groups was very recent and could have occurred quickly in small populations after only a few generations after the Tower of Babel, as groups of people spread throughout the different environments of the earth.

The rebellion of man at this critical moment in history, however, forever set these unique people groups against each other. Ethnic hatred, fighting, and "racism" have been the norm ever since. Man against man, nation against nation, the murder of Australian Aborigines, mockery of African pygmies, slavery of black Americans, slaughter of the Jews—the list goes on and on—and the only way humans can justify their evil actions is to abuse the truth about history, science, and the Word of God.

Abuse against fellow humans knows no boundaries. Over one hundred years ago, some Aborigines in Australia used "death shoes" to sneak up on their victims, usually at early dawn, to murder them. Sometimes the assassin was sent officially by the tribe; sometimes he acted out of private revenge. The death shoes, made of emu feathers, left no traceable track. The upper part of the shoe is made of human hair.

In the mid-nineteenth century, various distortions of the Bible and science were used to try to justify slavery. Some denied the biblical truth that all are descended from Adam and Eve. Others distorted what the Bible says to argue falsely that dark skin color was a curse upon Noah's son Ham.

Perhaps the most infamous abuse of evolution to justify racism was Adolf Hitler's Nazi regime, which promoted a master race and sought to exterminate so-called inferior races. Historian Arthur Keith described this particularly insidious harvest from Darwin's plantation with these words in the book *Evolution and Ethics*:

> To see evolutionary measures and tribal morality being applied rigorously to the affairs of a great modern nation, we must turn again to Germany of 1942. We see Hitler devoutly convinced that evolution provides the only real basis for a national policy. . . . The German Fuhrer, as I have consistently maintained, is an evolutionist; he has consciously sought to make the practice of Germany conform to the theory of evolution.[12]

Genocide as a state policy—such as in the Soviet Union, China, and Nazi Germany—has been condemned since the end of

World War II. The world saw the effects on "racism" through the lens of the Holocaust, but has human wisdom and effort been able to curtail it?

The word *racism,* of course, has its roots in *race,* the concept that there are distinct racial groups throughout the world: Asia, Europe, the Middle East, South America, and so on. But did you know that the concept of human races is not found in the Bible? The philosophy of racism, therefore, is alien to Scripture and originated with men.

In mid-19th-century England, "racism," or ethnic superiority, was quite popular. It also coincided with some of the most blatant attacks on the Bible as men like Herbert Spencer, Darwin, and Thomas Huxley sought to mythologize the Old Testament, starting, of course, with the creation account in Genesis.

Unfortunately, tragically, their views inspired men who would come after them and turn the 20th century into the bloodiest in all human history. Stalin, Hitler, and Mao were responsible for the deaths of tens of millions—and it can be shown that they did this because of the influence of Darwinian naturalism, which fanned the flames of ethnic superiority. According to human reason, everyone decides what is right in his own eyes. "Everyone did what was right in his own eyes" (Judges 21:25).

Once people abandon the authority of God's Word, there is no foundation for morality and justice in the world. When God's truth is rejected, human reason alone is used to justify evil of every sort.

- Racism

- Euthanasia

- Abortion

Rather than esteeming our brothers, we discriminate against them.

Rather than protecting our brothers, we hate them.

Rather than embracing our neighbors, we despise them.

Rather than protecting the helpless, we put ourselves first.

Without any absolute authority for right and wrong, humans in every generation have devised a multitude of excuses to justify abuse. Modern humans are no different. They have abused science to justify all sorts of evils. According to evolution, humans are nothing special:

- We have no Creator and are not accountable to anyone.

- Hominids evolved into many branches over millions of years.

- Death is a natural step in the cycle of life.

- We're just animals, and the fittest survive.

Even Stephen Jay Gould, a leading evolutionist, explains how people in the 19th century abused science to support their own prejudices:

> Biological arguments for racism may have been common before 1859, but they increased by orders of magnitude following the acceptance of evolutionary theory.[13]

Darwin's plantation—a pervasive and powerful root of racism—continues to spread throughout our culture and our world. It's not just part of our past; it continues throughout this generation. In some places there has been progress. In certain fields of our society racism is being rejected, and men and women are coming together as brothers and sisters.

In other parts of the world, racial and ethnic hatred continue to be unleashed in astronomical proportions. The evening news is a tale of man hating men because of the shade of color of their skin or the shape of their face.

Where will it end?

Certainly it will end at the second coming of Jesus Christ, when truth and order will be restored. But until then, what are we to do? How are we to live, think, and respond to our fellow humans on this planet? Is there any hope? I believe there is.

A survey of the history of racism will show us that these two solutions (biblical principles and scientific fact) are indispensable and powerful tools in uprooting Darwin's plantation and planting new seeds of truth in our hearts, our churches, and our world.

1. P.V. Bradford and H. Blume, *Ota Benga: The Pygmy in the Zoo* (New York: St. Martin's Press, 1992), pp. 113–114.

2. Jean-Pierre Hallet, *Pygmy Kitabu* (New York: Random House, 1973), pp. 14–15.

3. Ibid., pp. 118–119.

4. Ibid., p. 16.

5. Bradford and Blume, *Ota Benga: The Pygmy in the Zoo*, pp. 185–187.

6. Hallet, *Pygmy Kitabu*, pp. 292, 358–359.

7. Bradford and Blume, *Ota Benga: The Pygmy in the Zoo*, p. 304.

8. T.G. Crookshank, *The Mongol in Our Midst* (New York: E.F. Dutton, 1924).

9. From the foreword to *One Blood*, by Ken Ham (Green Forest, AR: Master Books).

10. David Monoghan, "The Body-Snatchers," *The Bulletin*, November 12, 1991.

11. Ibid., p. 33.

12. Arthur Keith, *Evolution and Ethics* (New York: G.P. Putnam's Sons, 1947), pp. 28–30, 230.

13. Stephen Jay Gould, *Ontogeny and Phylogeny* (Cambridge, MA: Belknap Press of Harvard University Press, 1977).

The Good News

I had gradually come, by this time, to see that the Old Testament from its manifestly false history of the world, with the Tower of Babel, the rainbow as a sign, etc., etc., from its attributing to God the feelings of a revengeful tyrant, was no more to be trusted than the sacred books of the Hindoos, or the beliefs of any barbarian.

—Charles Darwin,
The Autobiography of Charles Darwin

By the end of his life, Darwin had determined to reject what the Bible calls truth. There are rumors of a deathbed conversion, but those seem to be just rumors. Darwin equated the teachings of the Bible with any other religious text. By making these claims, Darwin was setting himself above God by saying that God's Word was wrong. To Darwin, man was the measure of all things and there was no need for God.

So what about you? What is your view of the teachings of the Bible? Regardless of what you have heard, have you ever read the Bible and examined the claims for yourself? If not, what is stopping you?

Darwin put his faith in his own reasoning and did not honor God with his life and his thinking. Could the same be said of you? If God is the Creator, as He claims in the Bible, then it only makes sense that He would set the standards for right and wrong. The Ten Commandments offer a summary of God's standard for what is right and wrong. The first commands that you should not elevate anything in your life above God (Exodus 20:3). The second commands that you should make no graven images to worship (Exodus 20:4–5). While you may not have a carved chunk of wood that you pray to, do you worship your money or yourself? Do you bow down to the television gods for hours each day? Where you spend your time and money reveals the things you desire to serve.

Have you ever murdered anyone? Chances are that you have not, but let's take a look at the heart of the matter. In Leviticus 19:17 we read "You shall not hate your brother in your heart," and in Zechariah 8:17 "Let none of you think evil in your heart against your neighbor . . . for all these are things that I hate,' says the Lord." Jesus also spoke on this topic in Matthew 5:22 saying "But I say to you that whoever is angry with his brother without a cause shall be in danger of judgment . . . ." While you may not have physically murdered anyone, have you ever harbored hatred against someone?

God also commands you to always tell the truth, to honor your parents, and to never desire something that is not yours (Exodus 20:1–17). If you honestly examine your life you must admit you have not lived up to God's standard of goodness. Most people would consider themselves to be good people when they compare themselves to the rest of the world. When we look at God's standard, we see a different picture.

Breaking God's laws is called sin and God takes it very seriously. He says that the punishment for sin is death (Romans 6:23). From the beginning of time, God has punished sinners for breaking His laws. Though we will all die physically, there is also an eternity after that. God's judgment against sin involves an eternal punishment in hell.

Since every human is a sinner (Romans 3:23), you might conclude that everyone deserves that punishment—and you would be correct. God's holiness and justice demands that the penalty for sin must be paid.

But there is good news! That doesn't have to be your eternal destination. Imagine you had just confessed your guilt before a judge and he handed down a $100 million fine. You can't pay the fine, nor could you ever pay it off. Then, as you are about to be ushered off to life in prison, a man steps out of the back of the courtroom and offers to pay your fine. That is exactly what Jesus Christ has done—He offers to pay the debt for your sins.

Jesus came to the earth as God in the flesh (John 1:1–14), lived a perfect life (committing no sins at all), died on the Cross, and then physically rose from the dead proving that He is the Savior and Lord of life. As Christ hung on the Cross, the wrath of God against sin was poured out on Him. This satisfied the justice of God and demonstrated His great mercy at the same time.

This offer of salvation from sin is made to all who will repent (confess their sins and turn from them) from their sins and put their trust in Christ as their Lord and Savior.

> "Now I rejoice, not that you were made sorry, but that your sorrow led to repentance. For you were made sorry in a godly manner, that you might suffer loss from us in nothing. For godly sorrow produces repentance *leading* to salvation, not to be regretted; but the sorrow of the world produces death." 2 Corinthians 7:9–10

> "For God so loved the world that He gave His only begotten Son, that whoever believes in Him should not perish but have everlasting life. For God did not send His Son into the world to condemn the world, but that the world through Him might be saved. He who believes in Him is not condemned; but he who does not believe is condemned already, because he has not believed in the name of the only begotten Son of God. And this is the condemnation, that the light has come into the world, and men loved darkness rather than light, because their deeds were evil. For everyone practicing evil hates the light and does not come to the light, lest his deeds should be ex-

posed. But he who does the truth comes to the light, that his deeds may be clearly seen, that they have been done in God." John 3:16–21

Charles Darwin left a legacy that includes a denial of what God reveals in the Bible. He rejected God as the Creator of life and placed his faith in his own ideas. Darwin saw change in the world around him and imagined the evolution of simple creatures into humans and all other life on earth. However, the Bible speaks of a more important kind of change—a spiritual change of the heart.

The change that you should seek in your life is the change from unrighteous sinner to someone who is forgiven by Christ. The apostle Paul describes this change from the old man to the new:

"Therefore, if anyone is in Christ, he is a new creation; old things have passed away; behold, all things have become new. Now all things are of God, who has reconciled us to Himself through Jesus Christ . . . ." 2 Corinthians 5:17–18

The old man is corrupt as a result of the sin brought into the world by Adam. Even as God pronounced a curse on Adam and all of creation, He also provided the promise of a "Seed" who would come (Genesis 3:15) to take away the penalty for that sin. Darwin called God's plan for justice and redemption revealed in the Bible a "damnable doctrine." Now that you know the truth revealed in Scripture, what will you call it?